Fundamental rights at work and international labour standards

Fundamental rights at work
and international labour standards

International Labour Office Geneva

Copyright © International Labour Organization 2003
First published 2003

Publications of the International Labour Office enjoy copyright under Protocol 2 of the Universal Copyright Convention. Nevertheless, short excerpts from them may be reproduced without authorization, on condition that the source is indicated. For rights of reproduction or translation, application should be made to the Publications Bureau (Rights and Permissions), International Labour Office, CH-1211 Geneva 22, Switzerland. The International Labour Office welcomes such applications.

Libraries, institutions and other users registered in the United Kingdom with the Copyright Licensing Agency, 90 Tottenham Court Road, London W1P 4LP [Fax: (+ 44) (0) 207 631 5500; email: cla@cla.co.uk], in the United States with the Copyright Clearance Center, 222 Rosewood Drive, Danvers, MA 01923 [Fax (+1) (978) 750 4470; email: info@copyright.com], or in other countries with associated Reproduction Rights Organizations, may make photocopies in accordance with the licences issued to them for this purpose.

ILO

Fundamental rights at work and international labour standards
Geneva, International Labour Office, 2003

Workers rights, freedom of association, collective bargaining, equal employment opportunity, forced labour, child labour, young worker, ILO convention, comment, application. 04.02.5

ISBN 92-2-113375-3

K
1705
.F86

ILO Cataloguing in Publication Data

The designations employed in ILO publications, which are in conformity with United Nations practice, and the presentation of material therein do not imply the expression of any opinion whatsoever on the part of the International Labour Office concerning the legal status of any country, area or territory or of its authorities, or concerning the delimitation of its frontiers.

The responsibility for opinions expressed in signed articles, studies and other contributions rests solely with their authors, and publication does not constitute an endorsement by the International Labour Office of the opinions expressed in them.

Reference to names of firms and commercial products and processes does not imply their endorsement by the International Labour Office, and any failure to mention a particular firm, commercial product or process is not a sign of disapproval.

ILO publications can be obtained through major booksellers or ILO local offices in many countries, or direct from ILO Publications, International Labour Office, CH-1211 Geneva 22, Switzerland. Catalogues or lists of new publications are available free of charge from the above address or by email: pubvente@ilo.org.

Photocomposed in Switzerland
Printed in Switzerland

WEI
PCL

CONTENTS

		page
1.	Introduction	1
2.	Freedom of association, *Bernard Gernigon, Alberto Odero and Horacio Guido*	5
	2.1 Introduction	5
	2.2 Content of the standards on freedom of association	6
	2.3 Summary of the principles of the Committee of Experts	13
	2.4 Application of standards and principles in practice	17
3.	Collective bargaining, *Bernard Gernigon, Alberto Odero and Horacio Guido*	21
	3.1 Introduction	21
	3.2 Content of the standards	22
	3.3 Summary of the principles of the Committee of Experts	28
	3.4 Application of the standards and principles in practice	30
4.	The abolition of forced or compulsory labour, *Max Kern and Carmen Sottas*	33
	4.1 Introduction	33
	4.2 The Forced Labour Convention, 1930 (No. 29)	34
	4.3 The Abolition of Forced Labour Convention, 1957 (No. 105)	45
5.	Equality of opportunity and treatment in employment and occupation, *Constance Thomas and Yuki Horii*	57
	5.1 Introduction	57
	5.2 Content of the standards on non-discrimination	60
	5.3 Summary of the principles of the Committee of Experts	72
	5.4 Practical difficulties and principal obstacles in the application of the Conventions	81

Fundamental rights at work and international labour standards

6. Protection of children and young persons,
   Ricardo Hernández-Pulido and Tania Caron 89
   6.1 Introduction 89
   6.2 The elimination of child labour 91
   6.3 Conditions of employment of young persons 113

Glossary 127

Bibliographical references and Internet sites 129

Tables
   2.1 Instruments on freedom of association 18
   3.1 Instruments on collective bargaining 31
   4.1 Instruments on the abolition of forced or compulsory labour 49
   5.1 Instruments on non-discrimination and equality of opportunity and
       treatment in employment and occupation 84
   6.1 Instruments on the elimination of child labour 118
   6.2 Instruments on the conditions of employment of young persons ... 120

INTRODUCTION

The concept of international labour standards is a fairly recent development in the context of world history. It was the Industrial Revolution in the nineteenth century and the related movement of ideas that served as a catalyst for the evolution of international human rights, and in particular of international labour standards. As the human cost of industrialization became apparent, there was increased awareness of the importance of protecting workers and establishing a universal set of international standards to ensure equal protection for all. In parallel, industrialists feared that they would lose out to competitors if they unilaterally improved working conditions. This led to the need for international social regulation in order to achieve a level playing-field for all parties.

The International Labour Organization (ILO) was established in 1919 with the aim of promoting social justice. The Declaration of Philadelphia of 1944 further specified and developed this approach. The main means of action was the adoption of international standards in the form of Conventions, which – similar to treaties – create obligations for member States once they have been ratified, and Recommendations. The principle that labour standards are an essential pillar of development and peace was enshrined in the ILO Constitution. The application of standards is seen as being vital for social stability, economic progress and lasting peace.

A unique element in the development of ILO standards, which sets them apart from other international standards, is the aspect of tripartitism. The participation of governments, along with the most representative workers' and employers' organizations, is an integral part of the ILO. Despite the sometimes conflictual nature of tripartitism, the participation of all three parties is necessary to find common ground for social and economic goals. Standards adopted through tripartitism result in a certain degree of dynamism and universality due to the fact that they are adopted by means of a process of consultation and result in a consensus of the diverse opinions of the various parties. As a result, the standards adopted are more adaptable to differing economic and social situations, while retaining all

Fundamental rights at work and international labour standards

their universality. At the same time, these human rights at work are closely interlinked with the full range of other human rights, which would lose much of their meaning without the solid basis of fundamental economic and social rights developed by the ILO.

It is important to emphasize the existence of international human rights law, which has been developed over the past 50 years and in which the ILO has played a vital role, even anticipating the series of international instruments and supervisory mechanisms which were established at both global and regional levels in the twentieth century. In 1919, the ILO Constitution established the right of association of workers and employers and the principle of equal remuneration for work of equal value, and in 1930 the 14th Session of the International Labour Conference (ILC) adopted the Forced Labour Convention (No. 29). In 1948, the United Nations adopted the Universal Declaration of Human Rights, which sets forth the major principles of human rights, although without developing them. Just a few months earlier, the ILC had adopted the Freedom of Association and Protection of the Right to Organise Convention (No. 87), governing the right of association of workers and employers. Prior to the United Nations International Covenants (1966), the ILC had already adopted other detailed Conventions on human rights: the Right to Organise and Collective Bargaining Convention, 1949 (No. 98); the Equal Remuneration Convention, 1951 (No. 100); the Abolition of Forced Labour Convention, 1957 (No. 105); and the Discrimination (Employment and Occupation) Convention, 1958 (No. 111). Recently, the Worst Forms of Child Labour Convention, 1999 (No. 182), has supplemented the protection afforded to children by the Minimum Age Convention, 1973 (No. 138).

Another prominent aspect of ILO standards is their system of enforcement through a multi-layered supervisory system, which is considered to be one of the most efficient at the international level. In order to ensure the application of standards in national law, a number of tools have been developed over the years. These include a regular supervisory system under which member States that have ratified Conventions are obliged to send in reports according to a periodic reporting schedule. The reports are examined by the Committee of Experts on the Application of Conventions and Recommendations (CEACR), an independent body consisting of 20 highly qualified independent experts in the legal or social fields. The tripartite Conference Committee on the Application of Standards then examines the CEACR's report. In addition, special supervisory tools exist for complaints containing specific allegations against a member State. These include the procedures set out in articles 24 and 26 of the ILO Constitution for cases of non-observance of the obligations deriving from a ratified Convention. Moreover, allegations concerning infringements of the principles of freedom of association may be made against governments, even if the country has not ratified the Conventions concerned.

At the end of the Cold War period in the late 1980s and early 1990s, the ILO felt the need to reassess its place in the changing global climate. It

Introduction

was decided that the ILO would give greater priority to promoting fundamental principles and rights. After some discussion, it was decided that eight Conventions concerning freedom of association, forced labour, equality of employment and opportunity, and child labour, were fundamental principles and rights that were either directly or indirectly contained in the ILO Constitution. Although these instruments were set apart from the others, the only legal change was the obligation to report every two years under the regular supervisory system, instead of every five years, as for most other Conventions.

The international labour standards concerning fundamental principles and rights and the ILO's supervisory system should be distinguished from the 1998 Declaration on Fundamental Principles and Rights at Work and its Follow-up. Even though the fundamental Conventions are an expression of the principles contained in the ILO Constitution, the Declaration, which is a promotional instrument, adopts a different approach. The Declaration's focus is on helping States to achieve compliance with the fundamental principles and rights through technical cooperation. In addition to technical cooperation, each year the ILO publishes a global report on one of the four fundamental principles, which serves as an assessment tool to improve the targeting of ILO technical cooperation, as well as a self-assessment tool for member States to see what progress has been made over a four-year period. The Declaration sets a decisive new benchmark, as it states that:

> ... all Members, even if they have not ratified the Conventions in question, have an obligation, arising from the very fact of membership in the Organization, to respect, to promote and to realize, in good faith and in accordance with the Constitution, the principles concerning the fundamental rights which are the subject of those Conventions, namely:
>
> (a) freedom of association and the effective recognition of the right to collective bargaining;
> (b) the elimination of all forms of forced or compulsory labour;
> (c) the effective abolition of child labour; and
> (d) the elimination of discrimination in respect of employment and occupation.

In the chapters that follow, the fundamental standards are examined along with other directly relevant standards. There is also a summary of the main principles of the CEACR. In addition, information is provided on the application of standards in practice and the main problems encountered in this respect. At the end of every chapter, a table shows the number of ratifications of the fundamental Conventions and other related Conventions, as well as the main decisions of the Governing Body on the status of these instruments (including the relevant Recommendations).

In conclusion, it should be emphasized that the main pillar of the notion of decent work, which is at the core of the ILO's strategy, is respect for fundamental rights at work. Indeed, this approach might otherwise be expressed

Fundamental rights at work and international labour standards

as "the *rights way* to decent work", with the inference that, while the problems and debates linked to globalization are not in any way new, they are now to be viewed more basically from the human rights perspective.

Jean-Claude Javillier
Director, International Labour Standards Department

FREEDOM OF ASSOCIATION

Bernard GERNIGON, Alberto ODERO
and Horacio GUIDO

2.1 INTRODUCTION

In its Preamble, the Constitution of the ILO (1919) affirms the principle of freedom of association as being among the means of improving the conditions of workers and ensuring peace. The 1944 Declaration of Philadelphia, which forms part of the Constitution of the ILO, affirms that "freedom of expression and of association are essential to sustained progress" and emphasizes that they are among the "fundamental principles on which the Organisation is based". In June 1998, the International Labour Conference adopted the ILO Declaration on Fundamental Principles and Rights at Work and its Follow-up, which states that "all Members, even if they have not ratified the [fundamental] Conventions (...), have an obligation, arising from the very fact of membership in the Organization, to respect, to promote and to realize, in good faith and in accordance with the Constitution, the principles concerning the fundamental rights which are the subject of those Conventions". These principles include freedom of association and the effective recognition of the right to collective bargaining. The Declaration considers as fundamental the principles of the Freedom of Association and Protection of the Right to Organise Convention, 1948 (No. 87), and the Right to Organise and Collective Bargaining Convention, 1949 (No. 98).

A summary of the relevant ILO instruments is given in table 2.1 on p. 18.

Freedom of association and collective bargaining are of vital importance for the social partners, since they enable them to establish rules in such areas as working conditions, including wages, and to further more general claims.

2.2 CONTENT OF THE STANDARDS ON FREEDOM OF ASSOCIATION

2.2.1 The right to organize, independence of organizations and non-interference by the authorities

The Freedom of Association and Protection of the Right to Organise Convention, 1948 (No. 87), applies to workers and employers and their organizations and sets forth the following rights and guarantees:

- Workers and employers, without distinction whatsoever, shall have the right to establish and, subject only to the rules of the organization concerned, to join organizations of their own choosing without previous authorization.
- Workers' and employers' organizations shall have the right to draw up their constitutions and rules, to elect their representatives in full freedom, to organize their administration and activities and to formulate their programmes. The public authorities shall refrain from any interference which would restrict this right or impede the lawful exercise thereof.
- Workers' and employers' organizations shall not be liable to be dissolved or suspended by administrative authority.
- The acquisition of legal personality by workers' and employers' organizations, federations and confederations shall not be made subject to conditions of such a character as to restrict the application of the above provisions.
- Workers' and employers' organizations shall have the right to establish and join federations and confederations. The above four provisions apply to federations and confederations of organizations of workers and employers.
- Any organization, federation or confederation shall have the right to affiliate with international organizations of workers and employers.
- In exercising the rights provided for in the Convention, workers and employers and their respective organizations, like other persons or organized collectivities, shall respect the law of the land. The law of the land shall not be such as to impair, nor shall it be so applied as to impair, the guarantees provided for in the Convention.
- The extent to which the guarantees provided for in the Convention shall apply to the armed forces and the police shall be determined by national laws or regulations.
- The term "organization" means any organization of workers or of employers for furthering and defending the interests of workers or of employers.

- Each Member of the International Labour Organization for which the Convention is in force undertakes to take all necessary and appropriate measures to ensure that workers and employers may exercise freely the right to organize.

2.2.2 Protection against acts of discrimination and interference

The Right to Organise and Collective Bargaining Convention, 1949 (No. 98), sets forth the following guarantees relating to the right to organize:[1]

- Workers shall enjoy adequate protection against acts of anti-union discrimination in respect of their employment.
  Such protection shall apply more particularly in respect of acts calculated to:
  - make the employment of a worker subject to the condition that he or she shall not join a union or shall relinquish trade union membership;
  - cause the dismissal of or otherwise prejudice a worker by reason of union membership or because of participation in union activities outside working hours, or with the consent of the employer, within working hours.
- Workers' and employers' organizations shall enjoy adequate protection against any acts of interference by each other or each other's agents or members in their establishment, functioning or administration.
  In particular, acts which are designed to promote the establishment of workers' organizations under the domination of employers or employers' organizations, or to support workers' organizations by financial or other means, with the object of placing such organizations under the control of employers or employers' organizations, shall be deemed to constitute acts of interference.

The Convention provides that "machinery appropriate to national conditions shall be established, where necessary, for the purpose of ensuring respect for the right to organize", as defined by the preceding provisions.

With regard to its scope of application, the Convention provides that the extent to which the guarantees for which it provides shall apply to the armed forces and the police shall be determined by national laws or regulations. Furthermore, the Convention does not deal with the position of public servants, nor shall it be construed as prejudicing their rights or status in any way.

2.2.3 Protection and facilities to be afforded to workers' representatives

The Workers' Representatives Convention, 1971 (No. 135), supplements the provisions of Convention No. 98 relating to anti-union discrimination since, although Convention No. 98 refers to the protection which shall be enjoyed by workers and trade union members, it does not specifically address the question of the protection of workers' representatives, nor the facilities necessary for them to carry out their functions.

For the purposes of Convention No. 135, these representatives may, in accordance with national law or practice, be representatives designated or elected by trade unions, or representatives who are freely elected by the workers of the enterprise (although in the latter case, their functions must not include activities that are recognized as the exclusive prerogative of trade unions). The type or types of representatives concerned may be determined through national laws or regulations, collective agreements, arbitration awards or court decisions.

With regard to the protection of workers' representatives in the enterprise, the Convention provides that they "shall enjoy effective protection against any act prejudicial to them, including dismissal, based on their status or activities as a workers' representative or on union membership or participation in union activities, in so far as they act in conformity with existing laws or collective agreements or other jointly agreed arrangements".

The Workers' Representatives Recommendation, 1971 (No. 143), lists as examples a number of measures with a view to affording effective protection against acts deemed to be prejudicial, including: detailed and precise definition of the reasons justifying termination of employment; consultation with, or an advisory opinion from, an independent or joint body; a special recourse procedure; an effective remedy for unjustified termination of employment including, unless this is contrary to the basic principles of the law of the country concerned, reinstatement with payment of unpaid wages and with maintenance of acquired rights; the laying upon the employer of the burden of proof; recognition of a priority to be given to workers' representatives with regard to their retention in employment in the case of reduction of the workforce. According to the Recommendation, the protection set out in the Convention should also apply to workers who are candidates for election or appointment as workers' representatives.

Convention No. 135 also provides that facilities in the enterprise shall be afforded to workers' representatives as may be appropriate in order to enable them to carry out their functions promptly and efficiently. In this connection, account has to be taken of the characteristics of the industrial relations system of the country and the needs, size and capabilities of the enterprise concerned. The Convention emphasizes that the granting of such facilities must not impair the efficient operation of the enterprise concerned.

Recommendation No. 143 lists a number of facilities for workers' trade union representatives, including: the granting of time off from work without loss of pay or benefits; access to workplaces, to the management of the enterprise and to management representatives empowered to take decisions; authorization to collect trade union dues; authorization to post trade union notices; distribution of union documents to workers; material facilities and information necessary for the exercise of their functions. The Recommendation envisages guarantees for employers that the facilities should not impair the efficient operation of the enterprise. It also envisages that elected representatives (of workers) should be given similar facilities as trade union representatives.

Effect may be given to the provisions of Convention No. 135 through national laws or regulations or collective agreements, or in any other manner consistent with national practice.

The Convention also states that "the existence of elected representatives" must not be "used to undermine the position of the trade unions concerned or their representatives" and, at the same time, that appropriate measures have to be taken to "encourage co-operation on all relevant matters between the elected representatives and the trade unions concerned and their representatives".

2.2.4 The right of association of rural workers' organizations

The Right of Association (Agriculture) Convention, 1921 (No. 11), provides that each Member which ratifies the Convention undertakes to "secure to all those engaged in agriculture the same rights of association and combination as to industrial workers, and to repeal any statutory or other provisions restricting such rights in the case of those engaged in agriculture". This protection is very limited in scope and it therefore appeared necessary to devote a specific instrument to rural workers.

The Rural Workers' Organisations Convention, 1975 (No. 141), associates rural workers' organizations with economic and social development for the permanent and effective improvement of their conditions of work and life.

Convention No. 141 applies to organizations of rural workers (including organizations not restricted to but representative of rural workers), to rural workers and wage earners and, subject to certain conditions, to tenant farmers, sharecroppers or small owner-occupiers, even if they are self-employed.

Convention No. 141 sets forth the right of rural workers to establish and join organizations of their own choosing with a view to participating in economic and social development and in the benefits resulting from it. These organizations must be independent, established on a voluntary basis,

Fundamental rights at work and international labour standards

and must remain free from all interference, coercion or repression. The Convention reaffirms the principles set out in Convention No. 87 concerning respect for law of the land and the acquisition of legal personality. In accordance with the Convention, member States are under the obligation to encourage the development of strong and independent organizations and to eliminate discrimination as an objective of national policy concerning rural development. Steps also have to be taken to promote the widest possible understanding of the need to further the development of these organizations and of the contribution that they can make.

The Rural Workers' Organisations Recommendation, 1975 (No. 149), develops the principles set out in Convention No. 141. It indicates that these organizations should represent rural workers and defend their interests, for instance through negotiations and consultations at all levels, including in relation to programmes of rural development and in national planning. The organizations should be associated with planning procedures and the functioning of the competent authorities.

The Recommendation emphasizes the role of organizations of rural workers in promoting their access to services such as credit and transport, in the improvement of education, training and conditions of work, and in the extension of social security and basic social services. It devotes several paragraphs to the principles of freedom of association, collective bargaining and protection against anti-union discrimination (including in relation to other workers and organizations), refers to the issue of the access of organizations to their members in a manner respecting the rights of all concerned, and recommends adequate machinery to ensure the implementation of laws and regulations.

The Recommendation advocates the adoption of appropriate measures to make possible the effective participation of such organizations in the formulation, implementation and evaluation of agrarian reform programmes.

The Recommendation also enumerates steps which should or might be taken to promote a better understanding of the contribution which can be made by rural workers' organizations in rural matters and the means of attaining this objective (information campaigns, seminars, etc.). Part of the Recommendation covers the training of the leaders and members of rural workers' organizations with a view to achieving the objectives that are indicated.[2]

Finally, Recommendation No. 149 indicates that financial and material assistance for rural workers' organizations, including that provided by the State, should be received in a manner which fully respects their independence and interests, and those of their members.

2.2.5 Trade union rights in the public administration

The Labour Relations (Public Service) Convention, 1978 (No. 151), was adopted taking into account the fact that Convention No. 98 does not cover certain categories of public servants and that the Workers' Representatives Convention, 1971 (No. 135), only applies to workers' representatives in the enterprise.

Convention No. 151 applies to all persons employed by public authorities (to the extent that more favourable provisions in other international labour Conventions are not applicable to them). However, it is for national laws or regulations to determine the extent to which the guarantees provided for in the Convention shall apply to: (1) high-level employees whose functions are normally considered as policy-making or managerial; (2) employees whose duties are of a highly confidential nature; and (3) the armed forces and the police.

Convention No. 151 contains similar provisions to those in Convention No. 98 concerning protection against anti-union discrimination and acts of interference, and to those in Convention No. 135 relating to the facilities to be afforded to representatives of organizations of public employees in order to enable them to carry out their functions promptly and efficiently (see above). With reference to these facilities, their nature and scope, the Labour Relations (Public Service) Recommendation, 1978 (No. 159), indicates that regard should be had to the Workers' Representatives Recommendation, 1971 (No. 143) (see above).

Convention No. 151 contains a provision on procedures for determining terms and conditions of employment which is analysed (alongside certain provisions of Recommendation No. 159) in Chapter 3, "Collective bargaining".[3]

Finally, Convention No. 151 provides that "public employees shall have, as other workers, the civil and political rights which are essential for the normal exercise of freedom of association, subject only to the obligations arising from their status and the nature of their functions".

2.2.6 Other categories of workers

The Migration for Employment Convention (Revised), 1949 (No. 97), lays down the principle of the non-discrimination of migrant workers in respect of "membership of trade unions and enjoyment of the benefits of collective bargaining". The Protection of Migrant Workers (Underdeveloped Countries) Recommendation, 1955 (No. 100), states that the right of association and freedom for all lawful trade union activities should be granted to migrant workers and that "all practicable measures should be taken to assure to trade unions which are representative of the workers concerned the right to conclude collective agreements". The Migrant Workers

Recommendation, 1975 (No. 151), reaffirms the principle of effective equality of opportunity and treatment with nationals in respect of membership of trade unions, exercise of trade union rights and eligibility for office in trade unions and in labour-management relations bodies, including bodies representing workers in enterprises.

The Indigenous and Tribal Peoples Convention, 1989 (No. 169), lays down that governments shall do everything possible to prevent any discrimination as regards "the right of association and freedom for all lawful trade union activities, and the right to conclude collective agreements with employers or employers' organisations".

The Plantations Convention, 1958 (No. 110), Parts IX and X, reproduces all the principles set out in Conventions Nos. 87 and 98.

The Merchant Shipping (Minimum Standards) Convention, 1976 (No. 147), is designed to ensure that States which have ratified it, for ships registered in their territory, ensure that the provisions of their laws and regulations are "substantially equivalent to the Conventions or Articles of Conventions referred to in the Appendix" to the Convention, which include Conventions Nos. 87 and 98.

The Merchant Shipping (Improvement of Standards) Recommendation, 1976 (No. 155), indicates that "steps should be taken, by stages if necessary, with a view to such laws or regulations, or as appropriate collective agreements, containing provisions at least equivalent to the provisions of the instruments referred to in the Appendix" to the Recommendation, which include the Workers' Representatives Convention, 1971 (No. 135).

2.2.7 Standards referring to strikes

Strikes are mentioned in the Abolition of Forced Labour Convention, 1957 (No. 105), and in the Voluntary Conciliation and Arbitration Recommendation, 1951 (No. 92). Convention No. 105 prohibits the use of any form of forced or compulsory labour "as a punishment for having participated in strikes" (Article 1(d)). Recommendation No. 92 advocates abstaining from strikes while conciliation or arbitration procedures (Paragraphs 4 and 6) are in progress and indicates that none of its provisions may be interpreted "as limiting, in any way whatsoever, the right to strike" (Paragraph 7).

2.3 SUMMARY OF THE PRINCIPLES OF THE COMMITTEE OF EXPERTS

The standards and principles concerning freedom of association derived from ILO Conventions and Recommendations, and the principles established by the Committee of Experts on the basis of these instruments, may be summarized as follows:

2.3.1 Trade union rights and civil liberties

- The guarantees set out in international labour Conventions, in particular those relating to freedom of association, can only be effective if the civil and political rights enshrined in the Universal Declaration of Human Rights and other international instruments are genuinely recognized and protected.

2.3.2 The right of workers and employers, without distinction whatsoever, to establish and join organizations of their own choosing

- The free exercise of this trade union right involves: the absence of any distinction (based on race, nationality, sex, marital status, age, political affiliation or activities) in law and in practice among those entitled to the right of association; the absence of the need for previous authorization to establish organizations; and freedom of choice with regard to membership of such organizations.
- The guarantees of Convention No. 87 should apply to all workers and employers without any distinction whatsoever, the only exceptions provided by the Convention being the armed forces and the police. Provisions prohibiting the right to organize for specific categories of workers, such as public servants, managerial staff, domestic staff or agricultural workers, are incompatible with the express provisions of the Convention.

2.3.3 The right to establish organizations without previous authorization

- The formalities required, such as those intended to ensure publicity, must not be so complex or lengthy as to give the authorities in practice discretionary power to refuse the establishment of organizations. Provision should be made for the possibility of a judicial appeal against any administrative decision of this kind to an independent and impartial body.

2.3.4 The right of workers and employers to establish and join organizations of their own choosing

- The right of workers and employers to establish organizations of their own choosing implies in particular the right to take freely the following decisions: choice of the structure and composition of organizations; the establishment of one or more organizations in any one enterprise, occupation or branch of activity; and the establishment of federations and confederations. It is derived from this principle that, although the Convention does not aim to make trade union pluralism compulsory, pluralism must be possible in every case, even if trade union unity was once adopted by the trade union movement. Systems of trade union unity or monopoly must not therefore be imposed directly by the law.
- Excessive restrictions as regards the minimum number of members are also incompatible with Article 2 of Convention No. 87.

2.3.5 Free functioning of organizations; the right to draw up their constitutions and rules

- In order for this right to be fully guaranteed, two basic conditions must be met: firstly, national legislation should only lay down formal requirements as regards trade union constitutions; secondly, the constitutions and rules should not be subject to prior approval at the discretion of the public authorities.
- The existence of a right to appeal to the courts in connection with the approval of by-laws does not in itself constitute a sufficient guarantee. The courts should be entitled to re-examine the substance of the case, as well as the grounds on which an administrative decision is based.

2.3.6 The right to elect representatives in full freedom

- The autonomy of organizations can be effectively guaranteed only if their members have the right to elect their representatives in full freedom. The public authorities should therefore refrain from any interference which might restrict the exercise of this right, whether as regards the holding of trade union elections, conditions of eligibility or the re-election or removal of representatives.
- The regulation of procedures and methods for the election of trade union officials is primarily to be governed by the trade unions' rules themselves. The fundamental idea of Article 3 of Convention No. 87 is that workers and employers may decide for themselves the rules which should govern the administration of their organizations and the elections which are held therein.

Freedom of association

- The intervention of the authorities in the exercise of this right should not go beyond provisions to promote democratic principles within trade unions or to ensure the proper conduct of the election process, with respect for members' rights, so as to avoid any dispute on their outcome.

2.3.7 The right of trade unions to organize their administration

- The right of workers' and employers' organizations to organize their administration without interference by the public authorities includes in particular autonomy and financial independence, and the protection of the assets and property of these organizations.
- Problems of compatibility with Convention No. 87 arise when the law establishes the minimum contribution of members, specifies the proportion of union funds that have to be paid to federations or requires that certain financial operations, such as the receipt of funds from abroad, be approved by the public authorities.
- Problems of compatibility also arise where the administrative authority has the power to examine the books and other documents of an organization, conduct an investigation and demand information at any time, or is the only body authorized to exercise control, or if such control is exercised by the single central organization expressly designated by the law.
- The freedom to organize their administration is not limited to strictly financial operations but also implies that trade unions should be able to dispose of all their fixed and movable assets unhindered and that they should enjoy inviolability of their premises, correspondence and communications.

2.3.8 The right of organizations to organize their activities in full freedom and to formulate their programmes

- This right includes in particular the right to hold trade union meetings, the right of trade union officers to have access to places of work and to communicate with management, certain political activities of organizations, the right to strike[4] and, in general, any activity involved in the defence of members' rights.
- The right to peaceful strike action must be recognized in general for trade unions, federations and confederations in the public and private sectors: this right may only be prohibited or subjected to important restrictions for the following categories of workers or in the following situations: members of the armed forces and the police; public servants exercising authority in the name of the State; workers in essential ser-

vices in the strict sense of the term (the interruption of which would endanger the life, personal safety or health of the whole or part of the population); and in the event of an acute national crisis.
- The conditions that have to be fulfilled under the law in order to render a strike lawful should be reasonable and in any event not such as to place a substantial limitation on the means of action open to trade union organizations.
- Appropriate protection should be afforded to trade union leaders and workers against measures which may be taken against them (dismissal or other sanctions) for organizing or participating in lawful and peaceful strikes.[5]

2.3.9 The right of workers' and employers' organizations to establish federations and confederations, and to affiliate with international organizations of workers and employers

- Workers' and employers' organizations should have the right to form federations and confederations of their own choosing, which should themselves enjoy the various rights accorded to first-level organizations, in particular as regards their freedom of operation, activities and programmes.
- International solidarity of workers and employers also requires that their national federations and confederations be able to group together and act freely at the international level.

2.3.10 Dissolution and suspension of organizations

- Measures of suspension or dissolution by the administrative authority constitute serious infringements of the principles of freedom of association.
- The dissolution and suspension of trade union organizations constitute extreme forms of interference by the authorities in the activities of organizations, and should therefore be accompanied by all the necessary guarantees. This can only be ensured through a normal judicial procedure, which should also have the effect of a stay of execution.
- As regards the distribution of trade union assets in the event of dissolution, these should be used for the purposes for which they were acquired.

Freedom of association

2.3.11 Protection against acts of anti-union discrimination

- The protection afforded to workers and trade union officials against acts of anti-union discrimination constitutes an essential aspect of freedom of association, since such acts may result in practice in denial of the guarantees laid down in Convention No. 87.
- Article 1 of Convention No. 98 guarantees workers adequate protection against acts of anti-union discrimination, in taking up employment and in the course of employment, including at the time of termination, and covers all prejudicial acts related to trade union membership or participation in lawful trade union activities.[6]
- The protection provided in the Convention is particularly important in the case of trade union representatives and officers, as these must have the guarantee that they will not be prejudiced on account of the union office which they hold.
- The existence of general legal provisions prohibiting acts of anti-union discrimination is inadequate unless they are combined with effective, expeditious, inexpensive and impartial procedures to ensure their application in practice, coupled with sufficiently dissuasive sanctions.
- Protection against acts of anti-union discrimination may take various forms adapted to national law and practice, provided that it prevents or effectively compensates anti-union discrimination.

2.3.12 Adequate protection against acts of interference

- The legislation should make express provision for rapid appeal procedures, coupled with effective and dissuasive sanctions against acts of interference by employers and their organizations against workers' organizations, and vice versa.

2.4 APPLICATION OF STANDARDS AND PRINCIPLES IN PRACTICE

Analysis of the content of the Committee of Experts' observations for 2000 and 2001 concerning the application of Convention No. 87 shows that comments were made for 88 of the 134 countries that have ratified the Convention. However, for most of these countries, the problems observed did not seriously impair the principles of freedom of association. The matters addressed include restrictions on the right of association of certain categories of workers (public servants, seafarers, workers in export processing zones, etc.) (40 countries). In a significant number of countries, the legisla-

Fundamental rights at work and international labour standards

Table 2.1 Instruments on freedom of association

Instruments	Number of ratifications (31 August 2002)	Status
Up-to-date instruments		(Conventions whose ratification is encouraged and Recommendations to which member States are invited to give effect.)
Freedom of Association and Protection of the Right to Organise Convention, 1948 (No. 87)	141	**Fundamental Convention.**
Workers' Representatives Convention, 1971 (No. 135)	72	The Governing Body has invited member States to contemplate ratifying Convention No. 135 and to inform the Office of any obstacles or difficulties encountered that might prevent or delay ratification of the Convention.
Workers' Representatives Recommendation, 1971 (No. 143)	–	The Governing Body has invited member States to give effect to Recommendation No. 143.
Rural Workers' Organisations Convention, 1975 (No. 141)	37	The Governing Body has invited member States to contemplate ratifying Convention No. 141 and to inform the Office of any obstacles or difficulties encountered that might prevent or delay ratification of the Convention.
Rural Workers' Organisations Recommendation, 1975 (No. 149)	–	The Governing Body has invited member States to give effect to Recommendation No. 149.
Other instruments		(This category comprises instruments that are no longer fully up to date but remain relevant in certain respects.)
Right of Association (Agriculture) Convention, 1921 (No. 11)	120	The Governing Body has invited the States parties to Convention No. 11 that have not yet ratified Convention No. 87 to contemplate doing so. In addition, it has invited member States that have not ratified either Convention No. 11 or Convention No. 87 to ratify the latter on a priority basis.
Right of Association (Non-Metropolitan Territories) Convention, 1947 (No. 84)	4	The Governing Body has invited member States that have made a formal commitment to apply the provisions of Convention No. 84 to contemplate ratifying Convention No. 87, and/or as appropriate, Convention No. 98. The Office has to conduct consultations on this issue with States parties to this Convention and inform the Governing Body of the result of the consultations.
Outdated instruments		(Instruments that are no longer up to date; this category includes the Conventions that member States are no longer invited to ratify and the Recommendations whose implementation is no longer encouraged.)
In the area of freedom of association, no instrument has been considered as outdated by the Governing Body.		

Freedom of association

tion contains restrictions on the categories of persons who may hold trade union office (distinction between nationals and foreigners) (15 countries), restrictions on the free election of trade union leaders (12 countries), the requirement of an excessive number of workers or employers to establish a trade union or an employers' association (11 countries), refusal to register organizations or the requirement of prior authorization (12 countries). Finally, there are a lower number of comments concerning the imposition by law of a trade union monopoly (eight countries), denial of the right to establish federations and confederations, or limitations on their functions (seven countries), dissolution of organizations by administrative authority (four countries) and the prohibition of more than one union in a single enterprise or sector (five countries). The comments also address restrictions on various aspects of the right to strike (the prohibition of this right for public servants other than those exercising authority in the name of the State, the imposition of compulsory arbitration, the prohibition of strikes in services that are not essential in the strict sense of the term, the denial of the right to strike for federations and confederations, and the imposition by the government of minimum services without consulting the parties).

In relation to the application of the provisions of Convention No. 98 respecting protection against acts of anti-union discrimination and interference, the observations of the Committee of Experts for 2000 and 2001 include critical comments concerning 34 of the 148 States that have ratified the Convention. The problems raised concern in particular legislation that does not contain provisions prohibiting anti-union discrimination (20 countries) or acts of interference (12 countries), or that provides inadequate protection, particularly in view of the absence of procedures (five countries) or of sufficiently dissuasive sanctions (12 countries). To a lesser extent, the problems raised concern the slowness of compensation procedures and the exclusion of certain categories of workers from the guarantees afforded by the Convention (five countries).

Notes

[1] The provisions of Convention No. 98 respecting collective bargaining are covered in Chapter 3.

[2] With regard to workers' education, reference should be made to other instruments. The Paid Educational Leave Convention, 1974 (No. 140), provides that each Member shall formulate and apply a policy designed to promote, by methods appropriate to national conditions and practice and by stages as necessary, the granting of paid educational leave for the purpose of (…) trade union education. The policy shall be designed to contribute, on differing terms as necessary:

(a) to the acquisition, improvement and adaptation of occupational and functional skills, and the promotion of employment and job security in conditions of scientific and technological development and economic and structural change;

(b) to the competent and active participation of workers and their representatives in the life of the undertaking and of the community;

(c) to the human, social and cultural advancement of workers; and

(d) generally, to the promotion of appropriate continuing education and training, helping workers to adjust to contemporary requirements.

Under the terms of the Convention, the financing of arrangements for paid educational leave shall be on a regular and adequate basis and in accordance with national practice.

The Paid Educational Leave Recommendation, 1974 (No. 148), indicates that the financing of arrangements for paid educational leave should be on a regular and adequate basis and in accordance with national practice. It adds that it should be recognized that employers, collectively or individually, public authorities and educational or training institutions or bodies, and employers' and workers' organizations, may be expected to contribute to the financing of arrangements for paid educational leave according to their respective responsibilities.

The Recommendation adds that the workers' organizations concerned should have the responsibility for the selection of candidates for trade union education. It also indicates that the manner in which workers who satisfy the conditions of eligibility are granted paid educational leave should be agreed upon between enterprises or the employers' organizations concerned and the workers' organizations concerned so as to ensure the efficient continuing operation of the enterprises in question.

Where trade union education programmes are carried out by the trade union organizations themselves, they should have the responsibility for planning, approval and implementation of the programmes. Where such programmes are carried out by other educational institutions or bodies, they should be established in agreement with the trade union organizations concerned.

Furthermore, the Human Resources Development Recommendation, 1975 (No. 150), provides that Members should aim in particular at establishing conditions permitting workers to supplement their vocational training by trade union education given by their representative organizations. The Recommendation advocates that representatives of employers' and workers' organizations should be included in the bodies responsible for governing publicly operated training institutions and for supervising their operations; where such bodies do not exist, representatives of employers' and workers' organizations should in other ways participate in the setting up, management and supervision of such institutions.

[3] Convention No. 151 also covers the settlement of collective labour disputes. This issue is also examined in Chapter 3.

[4] For the Committee of Experts, although the right to strike is not mentioned explicitly in Convention No. 87, it derives from Article 3, which sets forth the right of organizations to organize their activities and to formulate their programmes.

[5] For a complete overview of the principles of the supervisory bodies on the right to strike, see B. Gernigon, A. Odero and H. Guido: "ILO principles concerning the right to strike", in *International Labour Review*, Vol. 137, 1998, No. 4, pp. 441-481.

[6] For example, legislation which in practice allows employers to terminate employment of a worker, subject to the payment of the compensation provided for by the law in all cases of unjustified dismissal, when the real motive is the worker's trade union membership or activities, is inadequate under the terms of Article 1 of the Convention.

COLLECTIVE BARGAINING

Bernard GERNIGON, Alberto ODERO
and Horacio GUIDO

3

3.1 INTRODUCTION

One of the ILO's principal missions is to promote collective bargaining throughout the world. This mission was conferred upon it in 1944 by the Declaration of Philadelphia, which forms part of the Constitution of the ILO and which recognizes "the solemn obligation of the International Labour Organisation to further among the nations of the world programmes which will achieve [...] the effective recognition of the right of collective bargaining". This principle is set forth in the Right to Organise and Collective Bargaining Convention, 1949 (No. 98), which has since achieved almost universal adhesion in terms of ratifications, bearing witness to the force of the principles that it lays down in most countries.

A summary of the relevant ILO instruments is given in table 3.1 on p. 31.

More recently, in June 1998, the ILO took a further step by adopting the ILO Declaration on Fundamental Principles and Rights at Work and its Follow-up, which indicates that "all Members, even if they have not ratified the [fundamental] Conventions in question, have an obligation, arising from the very fact of membership in the Organization, to respect, to promote and to realize, in good faith and in accordance with the Constitution, the principles concerning the fundamental rights which are the subject of those Conventions". These principles include the effective recognition of the right to collective bargaining, as well as freedom of association.

Fundamental rights at work and international labour standards

3.2 CONTENT OF THE STANDARDS

3.2.1 Definition and purpose of collective bargaining

In the ILO's instruments, collective bargaining is deemed to be the activity or process leading up to the conclusion of a collective agreement. For the purposes of the Collective Agreements Recommendation, 1951 (No. 91), under Paragraph 2, the term "collective agreements":

> ... means all agreements in writing regarding working conditions and terms of employment concluded between an employer, a group of employers or one or more employers' organisations, on the one hand, and one or more representative workers' organisations, or, in the absence of such organisations, the representatives of the workers duly elected and authorised by them in accordance with national laws and regulations, on the other.

Also under the terms of Recommendation No. 91, collective agreements should bind the signatories thereto and those on whose behalf the agreement is concluded. Stipulations in contracts of employment which are contrary to a collective agreement should be regarded as null and void and be automatically replaced by the corresponding stipulations of the collective agreement. However, stipulations in contracts of employment which are more favourable to the workers than those prescribed by a collective agreement should be respected. Recommendation No. 91 therefore established in 1951 the principle of the binding nature of collective agreements and their precedence over individual contracts of employment, with the exception of clauses in such contracts that are more favourable for workers covered by the collective agreement.

Convention No. 98 does not contain a definition of collective agreements, but outlines their fundamental aspects in Article 4:

> Measures appropriate to national conditions shall be taken [...] to encourage and promote the full development and utilisation of machinery for voluntary negotiation between employers or employers' organisations and workers' organisations, with a view to the regulation of terms and conditions of employment by means of collective agreements.

In the preparatory work for the Labour Relations (Public Service) Convention, 1978 (No. 151), it was agreed that the term "negotiation" was to be interpreted as including "any form of discussion, formal or informal, that was designed to reach agreement", and that this word was preferable to "discussion", which "might not be designed to secure agreement".[1]

The Collective Bargaining Convention (No. 154), adopted in 1981, further defines this concept in Article 2:

> The term "collective bargaining" extends to all negotiations which take place between an employer, a group of employers or one or more employers' organisations, on the one hand, and one or more workers' organisations, on the other,

for: (a) determining working conditions and terms of employment; and/or (b) regulating relations between employers and workers; and/or (c) regulating relations between employers or their organizations and a workers' organisation or workers' organisations.

3.2.2 Subjects, parties and content of collective bargaining

The ILO's instruments authorize collective bargaining only with the representatives of the workers concerned in the absence of workers' organizations at the specific level (the enterprise or higher levels). This principle is set out in Paragraph 2, referred to above, of Recommendation No. 91 and is confirmed in the Workers' Representatives Convention, 1971 (No. 135), which provides in Article 5 that appropriate measures shall be taken to ensure that "the existence of elected representatives is not used to undermine the position of the trade unions concerned or their representatives". Similarly, Convention No. 154 provides in Article 3, paragraph 2, that "appropriate measures shall be taken, wherever necessary, to ensure that the existence of these [workers'] representatives is not used to undermine the position of the workers' organisations concerned".

The possibility for representatives of workers to be able to conclude collective agreements in the absence of one or various representative organizations of workers is envisaged in Recommendation No. 91, "taking into consideration the position of those countries in which trade union organisations have not yet reached a sufficient degree of development, and in order to enable the principles laid down in the Recommendation to be implemented in such countries".[2]

For trade unions to be able to fulfil their purpose of "furthering and defending the interests of workers" by exercising the right to collective bargaining, they have to be independent and must be able to organize their activities without any interference by the public authorities which would restrict this right or impede the lawful exercise thereof (Articles 3 and 10 of Convention No. 87). Furthermore, they must not be "under the control of employers or employers' organisations" (Article 2 of Convention No. 98). The Collective Bargaining Recommendation, 1981 (No. 163), provides that: "In so far as necessary, measures adapted to national conditions should be taken to facilitate the establishment and growth, on a voluntary basis, of free, independent and representative employers' and workers' organisations."

Convention No. 151 provides in Article 5 that "public employees' organisations shall enjoy complete independence from public authorities", and Recommendation No. 91 rejects any interpretation of collective bargaining "implying the recognition of any association of workers established, dominated or financed by employers or their representatives".

3.2.3 Requirement of a certain level of representativity

Another issue which should be examined is whether the right to negotiate is subject to a certain level of representativity.

In this respect, the Collective Bargaining Recommendation, 1981 (No. 163), enumerates various measures designed to promote collective bargaining, including the recognition of representative employers' and workers' organizations based on pre-established and objective criteria.

3.2.4 Preferential or exclusive bargaining rights

The Labour Relations (Public Service) Recommendation, 1978 (No. 159), indicates that in countries in which procedures for recognition of public employees' organizations apply with a view to determining the organizations to be granted, on a preferential or exclusive basis, the rights provided for under the Convention (and particularly collective bargaining), such determination should be based on objective and pre-established criteria with regard to the organizations' representative character.

3.2.5 Workers covered by collective bargaining

Convention No. 98 (Articles 4-6) associates collective bargaining with the conclusion of collective agreements for the regulation of terms and conditions of employment. It provides that "the extent to which the guarantees provided for in this Convention shall apply to the armed forces and the police shall be determined by national laws or regulations", and also states that "this Convention does not deal with the position of public servants engaged in the administration of the State".[3]

3.2.6 Subjects covered by collective bargaining

Conventions Nos. 98, 151 and 154, and Recommendation No. 91, focus the content of collective bargaining on terms and conditions of work and employment, and on the regulation of the relations between employers and workers and between organizations of employers and of workers.

3.2.7 The principle of free and voluntary negotiation

Article 4 of Convention No. 98 explicitly sets forth the voluntary nature of collective bargaining, which is a fundamental aspect of the principles of

Collective bargaining

freedom of association. The necessity to promote collective bargaining therefore excludes recourse to measures of compulsion. When the International Labour Conference was preparing Convention No. 154, it was agreed that no compulsory measures should be taken for this purpose.[4]

3.2.8 Free choice of collective bargaining

In this regard, Recommendation No. 163 indicates: "Measures adapted to national conditions should be taken, if necessary, so that collective bargaining is possible at any level whatsoever, including that of the establishment, the undertaking, the branch of activity, the industry, or the regional or national levels."

The ILO's standards have not established rigid criteria concerning the relationship between collective agreements at the different levels (which may address the economy in general, a sector or industry, an enterprise or group of enterprises, an establishment or factory; and which may, according to the individual case, have a different geographical scope). Paragraph 4 of Recommendation No. 163 states as follows: "In countries where collective bargaining takes place at several levels, the parties to negotiations should seek to ensure that there is co-ordination among these levels."

3.2.9 The principle of good faith

In the preparatory work for Convention No. 154, it was recognized that collective bargaining could only function effectively if it was conducted in good faith by both parties. However, as good faith cannot be imposed by law, it "could only be achieved as a result of the voluntary and persistent efforts of both parties".[5]

3.2.10 Voluntary procedures: Machinery to facilitate negotiations

Convention No. 154 encourages the establishment of rules of procedure agreed between employers' and workers' organizations. Nevertheless, the Conventions and Recommendations on collective bargaining admit conciliation and mediation that is voluntary or established by law, as well as voluntary arbitration, in accordance with the provisions of Recommendation No. 92, under which "provision should be made to enable the procedure to be set in motion, either on the initiative of any of the parties to the dispute or ex officio by the voluntary conciliation authority". Convention No. 154 clearly states that its provisions "do not preclude the operation of industrial relations systems in which collective bargaining takes place within the framework of conciliation and/or arbitration machinery or institutions, in which machinery or institutions the parties to the collective bargaining process voluntarily participate".

3.2.11 Interpretation and application of collective agreements

The Collective Agreements Recommendation, 1951 (No. 91), establishes that disputes arising out of the interpretation of a collective agreement should be submitted to an appropriate procedure for settlement established either by agreement between the parties or by laws or regulations as may be appropriate under national conditions. With regard to supervising the application of collective agreements, it establishes that such supervision should be ensured by the employers' and workers' organizations parties to such agreements or by the bodies existing or established for this purpose.

3.2.12 Settlement of disputes

Convention No. 151 provides as follows: "The settlement of disputes arising in connection with the determination of terms and conditions of employment shall be sought, as may be appropriate to national conditions, through negotiation between the parties or through independent and impartial machinery, such as mediation, conciliation and arbitration, established in such a manner as to ensure the confidence of the parties involved." The Collective Bargaining Convention, 1981 (No. 154), which is general in its scope, provides that bodies and procedures for the settlement of labour disputes should be so conceived as to contribute to the promotion of collective bargaining.

On this issue, the Collective Bargaining Recommendation, 1981 (No. 163), which is applicable to all branches of economic activity and to the public service, states: "Measures adapted to national conditions should be taken, if necessary, so that the procedures for the settlement of labour disputes assist the parties to find a solution to the dispute themselves, whether the dispute is one which arose during the negotiation of agreements, one which arose in connection with the interpretation and application of agreements or one covered by the Examination of Grievances Recommendation, 1967."

The Voluntary Conciliation and Arbitration Recommendation, 1951 (No. 92), encourages the parties concerned to abstain from strikes and lockouts while these procedures are in progress.

3.2.13 The right of information

Recommendation No. 163 indicates that: "measures adapted to national conditions should be taken, if necessary, so that the parties have access to the information required for meaningful negotiations", and adds: "Public and private employers should, at the request of workers' organisations, make available such information on the economic and social situation of the negotiating unit and the undertaking as a whole, as is necessary for meaningful negotiations; where the disclosure of some of this information could be prejudicial to the undertaking, its communication may be made conditional upon a commitment that it would be regarded as confidential to the extent required; the information to be made available may be agreed upon between the parties to collective bargaining." In addition, "the public authorities should make available such information as is necessary on the overall economic and social situation of the country and the branch of activity concerned, to the extent to which the disclosure of this information is not prejudicial to the national interest".

The Recommendation also advocates measures so that negotiators have the opportunity to receive appropriate training.

3.2.14 The extension of collective agreements

Recommendation No. 91 associates the representative organizations of workers and employers, and the employers and workers concerned, with the procedure of the extension of collective agreements.

3.2.15 Collective bargaining in the public service

The recognition of the right of collective bargaining for organizations of public officials and employees is now a reality in industrialized countries and is increasingly so in developing countries. Convention No. 98, adopted in 1949, excludes from its scope public servants engaged in the administration of the State. However, Convention No. 151, adopted in 1978, took an important step forward in requiring States to promote machinery for negotiation or such other methods as will allow representatives of public employees to participate in the determination of their terms and conditions of employment. Article 7 of Convention No. 151 provides that: "Measures appropriate to national conditions shall be taken, where necessary, to encourage and promote the full development and utilisation of machinery for negotiation of terms and conditions of employment between the public authorities concerned and public employees' organisations, or of such other methods as will allow representatives of public employees to participate in the determination of these matters." In accordance with Article 1 of the Convention, the only categories which may be excluded (in addition to the armed forces and the police, as in previous Conventions) are "high-level employees whose functions are normally considered as policy-making or managerial, or (...) employees whose duties are of a highly confidential nature".

Shortly afterwards, in 1981, Convention No. 154 was adopted. This Convention encourages collective bargaining in both the private sector and the public service (with the exception of the armed forces and the police), with the only reservation that national laws or regulations or national practice may fix "special modalities of application" of the Convention as regards the public service. Member States which ratify the Convention may no longer confine themselves to consultations. They are bound to promote collective bargaining for determining working conditions and terms of employment, among other objectives. The extension of the scope of Convention No. 154 to the public service was facilitated by the fact that, in contrast with Convention No. 98, this instrument does not refer to the determination of terms and conditions of employment by means of "collective agreements" (which have force of law in many countries, whereas agreements in the public sector *[accords collectifs, acuerdos colectivos]* do not have this binding force in certain countries). Such a provision would have rendered it impossible to extend the scope of the Collective Bargaining Convention, 1981 (No. 154), to the public service in view of the objections of the States which, although being prepared to recognize collective bargaining in the public service, were not ready to renounce the statutory system. Other indications of flexibility are also to be found in Convention No. 154 in its provision that "collective bargaining should be progressively extended to all matters covered" by the Convention or that its provisions shall, in so far as they are not otherwise made effective by means of collective agreements, arbitration awards or in such other manner as may be consistent with national practice, be given effect by national laws or regulations.

3.3 SUMMARY OF THE PRINCIPLES OF THE COMMITTEE OF EXPERTS

The standards and principles concerning the right to collective bargaining emerging from the ILO's Conventions, Recommendations and other relevant instruments, and the principles established by the Committee of Experts on the basis of these instruments, may be summarized as follows:

- The right to collective bargaining is a fundamental right endorsed by the Members of the ILO by the very fact of their membership of the Organization, which they have an obligation to respect, to promote and to realize in good faith (ILO Declaration on Fundamental Principles and Rights at Work and its Follow-up).

Collective bargaining

- Collective bargaining is a right of employers and their organizations, on the one hand, and organizations of workers, on the other hand (first-level trade unions, federations and confederations); only in the absence of these latter organizations may representatives of the workers concerned engage in collective bargaining.

- The right to collective bargaining should be recognized throughout the private and public sectors, and it is only the armed forces, the police and public servants engaged in the administration of the State who may be excluded from the exercise thereof (Convention No. 98).[6]

- The purpose of collective bargaining is the regulation of terms and conditions of employment, in a broad sense, and the relations between the parties.

- Collective agreements are binding on the parties and are intended to determine terms and conditions of employment which are more favourable than those established by law. Preference must not be given to individual contracts over collective agreements, except where more favourable provisions are contained in individual contracts.

- To be effective, the exercise of the right to collective bargaining requires that workers' organizations are independent and not under the control of employers or employers' organizations, and that the process of collective bargaining can proceed without undue interference by the authorities.

- A trade union which represents the majority or a high percentage of the workers in a bargaining unit may enjoy preferential or exclusive bargaining rights. However, in cases where no trade union fulfils these conditions or such exclusive rights are not recognized, workers' organizations should nevertheless be able to conclude a collective agreement on behalf of their own members.

- The principle of good faith in collective bargaining implies genuine and persistent efforts by both parties.

- In view of the fact that the voluntary nature of collective bargaining is a fundamental aspect of the principles of freedom of association, collective bargaining may not be imposed upon the parties and procedures to support bargaining must, in principle, take into account its voluntary nature. Moreover, the level of bargaining must not be imposed unilaterally by law or by the authorities, and it must be possible for bargaining to take place at any level.

- It is acceptable for conciliation and mediation to be imposed by law within the framework of the process of collective bargaining, provided that reasonable time limits are established. However, the imposition of compulsory arbitration in cases where the parties do not reach agreement is generally contrary to the principle of voluntary collective bargaining and is only admissible: (1) in essential services in the strict sense of the term (those whose interruption would endanger the life, personal safety or health of the whole or part of the population); (2) with regard to public servants engaged in the administration of the State; (3) where, after prolonged and fruitless negotiations, it is clear that the deadlock will not be overcome without an initiative by the authorities; and (4) in the event of an acute national crisis. Arbitration which is accepted by both parties (voluntary arbitration) is always legitimate.

- Interventions by the legislative or administrative authorities which have the effect of annulling or modifying the content of freely concluded collective agreements, including wage clauses, are contrary to the principle of voluntary collective bargaining.

- Restrictions on the content of future collective agreements, particularly in relation to wages, which are imposed by the authorities as part of economic stabilization or structural adjustment policies for imperative reasons of economic interest, are admissible only in so far as such restrictions are preceded by consultations with the organizations of workers and employers and fulfil the following conditions: they are applied as an exceptional measure, and only to the extent necessary; they do not exceed a reasonable period; and they are accompanied by adequate guarantees designed to protect effectively the standards of living of the workers concerned, and particularly those who are likely to be the most affected.

3.4 APPLICATION OF THE STANDARDS AND PRINCIPLES IN PRACTICE

The observations made by the Committee of Experts concerning the application of the Right to Organise and Collective Bargaining Convention, 1949 (No. 98), show that the great majority of States which have ratified the Convention apply it in a satisfactory manner. This demonstrates that it is a right which enjoys almost universal recognition in law and practice.

In this respect, in its reports for 2000 and 2001, the Committee of Experts made critical observations to one-third of the 148 governments that have ratified Convention No. 98. The problems which arise most frequently concern the denial of the right of collective bargaining to all public servants or to public servants who are not engaged in the administration of the State (19 countries) and the requirement for trade union organizations to represent too high a proportion of workers to be recognized or to engage in collective bargaining (11 countries). These are followed by the fact that in a significant number of countries collective bargaining is subordinated to the government's economic policy (eight countries). Finally, certain countries exclude certain subjects from collective bargaining (six countries), submit it

Collective bargaining

Table 3.1 Instruments on collective bargaining

Instruments	Number of ratifications (31 August 2002)	Status
Up-to-date instruments (Conventions whose ratification is encouraged and Recommendations to which member States are invited to give effect.)		
Right to Organise and Collective Bargaining Convention, 1949 (No. 98)	152	**Fundamental Convention.**
Labour Relations (Public Service) Convention, 1978 (No. 151)	39	The Governing Body has invited member States to contemplate ratifying Convention No. 151 and to inform the Office of any obstacles or difficulties encountered that might prevent or delay ratification of the Convention.
Labour Relations (Public Service) Recommendation, 1978 (No. 159)	–	The Governing Body has invited member States to give effect to Recommendation No. 159.
Collective Bargaining Convention, 1981 (No. 154)	33	The Governing Body has invited member States to contemplate ratifying Convention No. 154 and to inform the Office of any obstacles or difficulties encountered that might prevent or delay ratification of the Convention.
Collective Bargaining Recommendation, 1981 (No. 163)	–	The Governing Body has invited member States to give effect to Recommendation No. 163.
Collective Agreements Recommendation, 1951 (No. 91)	–	The Governing Body has invited member States to give effect to Recommendation No. 91.
Outdated instruments (Instruments that are no longer up to date; this category includes the Conventions that member States are no longer invited to ratify and the Recommendations whose implementation is no longer encouraged.)		
In the area of collective bargaining, no instrument has been considered as outdated by the Governing Body.		

to compulsory arbitration in certain cases (six countries), restrict the right of the parties to determine the level of bargaining (three countries), and prohibit collective bargaining by specific categories of workers in the private sector (two countries) or by federations and confederations (four countries).

Notes

[1] ILO: *Record of Proceedings*, International Labour Conference, 64th Session, Geneva, 1978, *Provisional Record* No. 25, p. 25/9, paras. 64 and 65.

[2] ILO: *Record of Proceedings*, International Labour Conference, 34th Session, Geneva, 1951, Appendix VIII, p. 603, para. 75.

[3] With regard to this category of public servants, the Committee of Experts has indicated that it "could not allow the exclusion from the terms of the Convention of large categories of workers employed by the State merely on the grounds that they are formally placed on the same footing as public officials engaged in the administration of the State. The distinction must therefore be drawn between, on the one hand, public servants who by their functions are directly employed in the administration of the State (for example, in some countries, civil servants employed in government ministries and other comparable bodies, as well as ancillary staff) who may be excluded from the scope of the Convention and, on the other hand, all other persons employed by the government, by public enterprises or by autonomous public institutions, who should benefit from the guarantees provided for in the Convention". ILO: *Freedom of association and collective bargaining,* General Survey of the Reports on the Freedom of Association and Protection of the Right to Organise Convention, 1948 (No. 87), and the Right to Organise and Collective Bargaining Convention, 1949 (No. 98), Report of the Committee of Experts on the Application of Conventions and Recommendations, Report III (Part 4B), International Labour Conference, 81st Session, Geneva, 1994, para. 200.

[4] ILO: *Record of Proceedings,* International Labour Conference, 67th Session, p. 22/6, Geneva, 1981, *Provisional Record* No. 22, p. 22/6, para. 49.

[5] ibid., p. 22/11, para. 91.

[6] Nevertheless, when a State ratifies the Collective Bargaining Convention, 1981 (No. 154), the right to collective bargaining is also applicable in the context of the public administration, for which special modalities of application may be fixed. In contrast, the Labour Relations (Public Service) Convention, 1978 (No. 151), permits, in the context of the public administration, the possibility of choosing between collective bargaining and other methods for the determination of terms and conditions of employment.

THE ABOLITION OF FORCED OR COMPULSORY LABOUR

Max KERN and Carmen SOTTAS

4.1 INTRODUCTION

In the present-day world, forced or compulsory labour is being imposed for the purpose of production or service and as a sanction or corollary of punishment. It is exacted by the State or by private persons or entities, under national laws and regulations or illegally, openly or hidden from the public view.

In principle, forced or compulsory labour is almost universally banned. The two ILO Conventions dealing with the abolition of forced or compulsory labour are the most widely ratified of its Conventions: as of 31 August 2002, the Forced Labour Convention, 1930 (No. 29), had been ratified by 161 States and the Abolition of Forced Labour Convention, 1957 (No. 105), had received 158 ratifications.

A summary of the relevant ILO instruments is given in table 3.1 on p. 49.

Moreover, the ILO Declaration on Fundamental Principles and Rights at Work, adopted by the International Labour Conference at its 86th Session, in 1998:

> Declares that all members, even if they have not ratified the Conventions in question, have an obligation, arising from the very fact of membership in the Organization, to respect, to promote and to realize, in good faith and in accordance with the Constitution, the principles concerning the fundamental rights which are the subject of those Conventions, namely: ... the elimination of all forms of forced or compulsory labour ...

The fundamental requirements of the two Conventions are considered below.

4.2 THE FORCED LABOUR CONVENTION, 1930 (NO. 29)

The main provisions of the Forced Labour Convention, 1930 (No. 29), are examined as follows: measures called for under Article 1, paragraph 1, and Article 25 of the Convention; definition of forced or compulsory labour (Article 2, paragraph 1); exceptions from the scope of the Convention (Article 2, paragraph 2); and present status of Article 1, paragraph 2, and Articles 4-24 of the Convention.

4.2.1 Measures called for under Articles 1, paragraph 1 and 25, of the Convention

The basic obligation undertaken by a State which ratifies the Forced Labour Convention, 1930 (No. 29), is "to suppress the use of forced or compulsory labour in all its forms within the shortest possible period".[1] This obligation to suppress the use of forced or compulsory labour, as defined in the Convention,[2] includes for the State both an obligation to abstain and an obligation to act. The State must neither exact forced or compulsory labour nor tolerate its exaction and it must repeal any laws and statutory or administrative instruments that provide or allow for the exaction of forced or compulsory labour, so that any such exaction, be it by private persons or public servants, is found illegal in national law.

Furthermore, the State must ensure that "the illegal exaction of forced or compulsory labour shall be punishable as a penal offence" and "that the penalties imposed by law are really adequate and are strictly enforced" (see box on facing page).[3]

4.2.2 Definition of forced or compulsory labour

The Convention defines "forced or compulsory labour" as "all work or service which is exacted from any person under the menace of any penalty and for which the said person has not offered himself voluntarily".[4] Before setting out the express exceptions retained in the Convention,[5] three aspects of this definition need to be considered so as to ascertain the general scope of the Convention: the notion of "work or service"; the "menace of any penalty"; and the criteria for not having "offered oneself voluntarily".[6]

(a) Work or service

In the first place, the definition refers to "work or service". As noted by the Committee of Experts on the Application of Conventions and Recommendations,[7] the exaction of work or service may be distinguished from cases in which an obligation is imposed to undergo education or training. The principle of compulsory education is recognized in various international standards

The abolition of forced or compulsory labour

> In order to effectively suppress the use of forced or compulsory labour and ensure that adequate penalties are not only provided for by law but also strictly enforced, the measures to be taken must take account of the nature of the problems which may arise in practice. Thus, with regard to the trafficking in persons for the purpose of exploitation, the Committee of Experts has sought information, inter alia, on measures taken to ensure that the provisions of national legislation aimed at the punishment of the exaction of forced or compulsory labour, trafficking in persons and the exploiters of the prostitution of others:
>
> ... are strictly enforced against those responsible for the forced labour of legal or illegal migrants, inter alia, in sweatshops, prostitution, domestic service and agriculture; in particular, measures required in practice for court proceedings to be initiated and completed, including:
>
> (a) measures designed to encourage the victims to turn to the authorities, such as:
>   (i) permission to stay in the country at least for the duration of court proceedings, and possibly permanently;
>   (ii) efficient protection of victims willing to testify and of their families from reprisals by the exploiters both in the country of destination and the country of origin of the victim, before, during and after any court proceedings, and beyond the duration of any prison term that might be imposed on the exploiter; and the participation of the government in any forms of intergovernmental cooperation set up for this purpose;
>   (iii) measures designed to inform victims and potential victims of trafficking of measures under (i) and (ii), with due regard to any barriers of language and circumstances of physical confinement of victims;
>
> (b) measures designed to strengthen the active investigation of organized crime with regard to trafficking in persons, the exploitation of the prostitution of others, and the running of sweatshops, including:
>   (i) the provision of adequate material and human resources to law enforcement agencies;
>   (ii) the specific training of law enforcement officers, including those working in immigration control, labour inspection and vice squads, to address the problems of trafficking in persons in a manner conducive to the arrest of the exploiters rather than of the victims;
>   (iii) international cooperation between law enforcement agencies with a view to preventing and combating the trafficking in persons;
>
> (c) cooperation with employers' and workers' organizations as well as non-governmental organizations engaged in the protection of human rights and the fight against the trafficking in persons, with regard to matters considered under ... (a) and (b)(ii) ....*
>
> ———
> * ILO: *Report of the Committee of Experts on the Application of Conventions and Recommendations*, Report III (Part 1A), International Labour Conference (ILC), 89th Session, 2001, general observation, Convention No. 29.

as a means of securing the right to education,[8] and it is also provided for in several ILO instruments.[9] A similar distinction is to be found in other international labour standards between work and vocational training.[10] The Committee of Experts has also pointed out that a compulsory scheme of vocational training, by analogy with and considered as an extension to compulsory general education, does not constitute compulsory work or service within the meaning of the Forced Labour Convention, 1930 (No. 29).[11] "However, as vocational training usually entails a certain amount of practical work, the distinction between training and employment is not always easy to draw. It is by reference to the various elements involved in the general context of a particular scheme of training that one may determine whether it is unequivocally one of vocational training, or on the contrary involves the exaction of work or service within the definition of 'forced or compulsory labour'."[12]

(b) Menace of any penalty

To fall within the definition of "forced or compulsory labour" in the 1930 Convention, work or service must be exacted "under the menace of any penalty". It was made clear during the consideration of the draft instrument by the Conference that the penalty here in question need not be in the form of penal sanctions, but might take the form also of a loss of rights or privileges.[13] For example, for a prisoner, it may consist of being placed at a lower level of privileges,[14] or of a reduced prospect of early release.[15]

(c) Voluntary offer

In considering the issue of "voluntary offer", the ILO supervisory bodies have touched upon a certain number of different aspects: the form and subject matter of the consent; the role of external or indirect constraints for which the State or the employer may be accountable or not; the possibility for a minor (or his or her parents) to give a valid consent; and the possibility of revoking a freely given consent.

(i) Form and subject matter of consent

The Convention does not prescribe the modalities of expressing agreement to work and the ILO supervisory bodies have sought to ascertain formal consent (whatever its modalities) merely in specific circumstances where the free will of the worker cannot be taken for granted and, in particular, where a prisoner performs work which may not be exacted from him or her under the Convention.[16]

As regards the subject matter of consent, seeking employment must be distinguished from accepting a concrete position: thus, where migrant workers were induced by deceit, false promises and retention of identity documents or force to remain at the disposal of an employer, the ILO supervisory bodies noted a violation of the Convention.[17]

(ii) The role of external constraints or indirect coercion

In considering the freedom to "offer oneself voluntarily" for work or service, account must be taken of the legislative and practical framework guaranteeing or limiting that freedom: thus, the mere freedom to choose among any type of work or service is not sufficient to ensure observance of the Convention where national law provides for a general obligation to work, i.e. makes it a legal obligation for all able-bodied citizens who are not receiving some kind of instruction to engage in a gainful occupation. This has been found incompatible with the 1930 and 1957 Conventions.[18]

The abolition of forced or compulsory labour

Similarly, where captive labour – such as persons called up for compulsory military service, or serving a prison term – are being offered a limited choice between work which can anyway be exacted under the exceptions provided for in the Convention, and some other work which is being offered to them and which does not fall under those exceptions,[19] the altogether relative freedom of choice is not in itself sufficient for considering acceptance of the work offered as being freely consented to.[20]

An external constraint or indirect coercion interfering with a worker's freedom to "offer himself voluntarily" may result not only from an act of the authorities, such as a statutory instrument, but also from an employer's practice, such as retention of a migrant worker's identity documents;[21] in the latter case, the State's responsibility is also involved under the Convention.[22] However, the employer or the State are not accountable for all external constraints or indirect coercion existing in practice; for example, the need to work in order to earn one's living could become relevant only in conjunction with other factors for which they are answerable. Such factors might be, for example, legislation under which persons requesting asylum are normally prohibited from taking up employment, but the very same persons may be called upon to perform "socially useful work" which they have no choice but to carry out if they are to maintain their welfare entitlements.[23]

In order to establish to what extent the State is accountable for an economic constraint, the ILO supervisory bodies have resorted to the following criteria:

> In a case where an objective situation of economic constraint exists but has not been created by the Government, then only if the Government exploits that situation by offering an excessively low level of remuneration could it to some extent become answerable for a situation that it did not create. Moreover, it might be held responsible for organizing or exacerbating economic constraints if the number of people hired by the Government at excessively low rates of pay and the quantity of work done by such employees had a knock-on effect on the situation of other people, causing them to lose their normal jobs and face identical economic constraints.[24]

(iii) Possibility for a minor (or his or her parents) to give valid consent

As was noted by the ILO supervisory bodies with regard to child labour, the question arises whether, and if so, under what circumstances, a minor can be considered to have offered himself or herself "voluntarily" for work or service and whether the consent of the parents is needed in this regard and whether it is sufficient, and what the sanctions for refusal are.[25] Most national legal orders, while fixing the coming of age as a rule somewhere between 18 and 21 years of age, have established, for the purposes of concluding a labour contract, a lower age limit, which may coincide with the age at which compulsory school attendance ends; but employment that is likely to jeopardize health, safety or morals is generally prohibited for persons below 18 years of age, in conformity with the relevant ILO Conventions,[26] so that neither they nor those having parental authority over them may give valid consent to their admission to such employment.[27] The ILO supervisory bodies have regularly raised cases of exploitation of children under the Forced Labour Convention, 1930 (No. 29),[28] but have also requested – and obtained – that minors engaged in a military career could terminate their engagement.[29]

(iv) Possibility of revoking a freely given consent

Once an adult has "offered himself – or herself – voluntarily" for some work or service, the latter does not come under the strict definition of forced or compulsory labour given in Article 2, paragraph 1, of the Convention; but does it follow from such freely given consent that any restrictions on workers' freedom to leave their employment will remain outside the scope of the Convention? The ILO supervisory bodies have considered that, although in such cases employment is originally the result of a freely concluded agreement, the workers' right to free choice of employment remains inalienable. Accordingly, the effect of statutory provisions preventing termination of employment of indefinite duration (or very long duration) by means of notice of reasonable length is to turn a contractual relationship based on the will of the parties into service by compulsion of law, and is thus incompatible with the Conventions relating to forced labour. This is also the case when a worker is required to serve beyond the expiry of a contract of fixed duration.[30]

The ILO supervisory bodies have thus addressed restrictions on the freedom to leave one's employment by giving notice of reasonable length that were imposed in different countries, in particular on professional soldiers,[31] on all persons in government service[32] or in the socialist and mixed sectors,[33] or even on all workers.[34]

4.2.3 Exceptions from the scope of the Convention (Article 2, paragraph 2)

By virtue of Article 2, paragraph 2, of the Convention, certain forms of compulsory service which would otherwise have fallen under the general definition of "forced or compulsory labour" are excluded from its scope "for the purposes of this Convention":

(a) any work or service exacted in virtue of compulsory military service laws for work of a purely military character;

(b) any work or service which forms part of the normal civic obligations of the citizens of a fully self-governing country;

(c) any work or service exacted from any person as a consequence of a conviction in a court of law, provided that the said work or service is carried out under the supervision and control of a public authority and that the

The abolition of forced or compulsory labour

said person is not hired to or placed at the disposal of private individuals, companies or associations;

(d) any work or service exacted in cases of emergency, that is to say, in the event of war or of a calamity or threatened calamity, such as fire, flood, famine, earthquake, violent epidemic or epizootic diseases, invasion by animal, insect or vegetable pests, and in general any circumstance that would endanger the existence or the well-being of the whole or part of the population;

(e) minor communal services of a kind which, being performed by the members of the community in the direct interest of the said community, can therefore be considered as normal civic obligations incumbent upon the members of the community, provided that the members of the community or their direct representatives shall have the right to be consulted in regard to the need for such services.

The conditions laid down by these provisions which define the limits of the exceptions are considered below.

(a) Compulsory military service

Convention No. 29 exempts from its provisions compulsory military service, provided that it is used "for work of a purely military character".[35] The condition of a "purely military character", aimed specifically at preventing the call-up of conscripts for public works,[36] has its corollary in Article 1(b) of the Abolition of Forced Labour Convention, 1957 (No. 105), which prohibits the use of forced or compulsory labour "as a means of mobilizing and using labour for purposes of economic development".[37]

There are, however, specific circumstances in which a non-military activity performed within the framework of compulsory military service or as an alternative to such service remains outside the scope of the forced labour Convention.[38] In the first place, conscripts, as any other citizens, may be called to work in cases of emergency, as defined in the Convention.[39] Also, conscripts performing their service in engineering or similar units may be made to join in the building of roads and bridges as a part of their military training.

Lastly, while the Convention does not mention the issue of conscientious objectors, the ILO supervisory bodies have considered that their exemption from compulsory military service, coupled with an obligation to perform an alternative service, is a privilege granted to individuals on request, in the name of freedom of conscience. But more generally, the existence of a choice between military service proper and non-military work does not in itself exclude the application of the Convention when the choice between different forms of service is made within the framework and on the basis of a compulsory service obligation. The number of persons concerned and the conditions in which they make their choice thus need, inter alia, to be taken into account in examining whether a privilege was granted to individuals on request or whether, on the contrary, national service becomes a means of pursuing economic and social development with the use of compulsory labour.[40]

(b) Normal civic obligations

"Any work or service which forms part of the normal civic obligations of the citizens of a fully self-governing country" is exempted from the scope of the Convention.[41]

Examples are compulsory jury service and the duty to assist a person in danger.[42] Other "normal civic obligations" are specifically mentioned in the Convention which limits their scope: compulsory military service in the conditions set out above,[43] as well as assistance in cases of emergency[44] and "minor communal services".[45] The ILO supervisory bodies have noted that the general reference to "normal civic obligations" must be read in the light of the other provisions of the Convention and cannot be invoked to justify recourse to forms of compulsory service which are contrary to the specific conditions laid down in those other provisions.[46]

(c) Prison labour

The Convention exempts from its provisions "any work or service exacted from any person as a consequence of a conviction in a court of law, provided that the said work or service is carried out under the supervision and control of a public authority and that the said person is not hired to or placed at the disposal of private individuals, companies or associations".[47] Compulsory prison labour thus is excluded from the scope of the Convention only if a certain number of conditions are met, some of which concern the basis for the obligation to work and others the conditions in which penal labour may be used.

(i) Basis for the obligation to work

The consequence of a conviction

The Convention provides that work can only be exacted from a prisoner as a consequence of a conviction. It follows that persons who are in detention but have not been convicted – such as prisoners awaiting trial or persons detained without trial – should not be obliged to perform labour. It also follows from the use of the term "conviction" that the person concerned must have been found guilty of an offence. In the absence of such a finding of guilt, compulsory labour may not be imposed, even as a result of a decision by a court of law.[48]

Conviction in a court of law

According to the Convention, work can only be exacted from a person as a consequence of a conviction "in a court of law". It follows that compulsory labour imposed by administrative or other non-judicial bodies or authorities is not compatible with the Convention. This provision aims at ensuring that penal labour will not be imposed unless the guarantees laid down in the general principles of law recognized by the community of nations are observed, such as the presumption of innocence, equality before the law, regularity and impartiality of proceedings, independence and impartiality

The abolition of forced or compulsory labour

of courts, guarantees necessary for defence, clear definition of the offence and non-retroactivity of penal law.[49]

(ii) Conditions governing the use of compulsory prison labour

Under the terms of the Convention, compulsory prison labour must be "carried out under the supervision and control of a public authority", and the prisoner must not be "hired to or placed at the disposal of private individuals, companies or associations".[50] The two conditions are cumulative and apply independently; the fact that the prisoner remains at all times under the supervision and control of a public authority does not in itself dispense the government from fulfilling the second condition, namely that the person is not hired to or placed at the disposal of private individuals, companies or associations.[51]

Supervision and control of a public authority

If the supervision and control are restricted to a general authority to inspect the premises periodically, this by itself would not appear to meet the requirements of the Convention for supervision and control.[52]

Meaning of the terms "hired to" or "placed at the disposal of"

Hired to. The normal meaning of the term "hired to" as understood at the time of the adoption of the Convention can be seen in the description of the lease system, the general contract system and the special contract system given in the Memorandum of 1931 of the International Labour Office "on such of the problems of prison administration as are within its competence, i.e. those relating to prison labour":[53]

> Contract labour is one of the older systems of prison labour; it still exists in some countries.
>
> The term denotes systems in which the labour of the prisoners is hired out to private contractors (private persons, companies or associations). These systems comprise:
>
> (a) *The Lease System*. This system is based on a contract between the State and a contractor, under which the prisoners are hired out to the latter, who is often styled the lessee. His contractual obligations are the boarding, lodging, clothing, and guarding of the prisoners, and the payment of an agreed per capita rate, in return for which he acquires the right to employ the prisoners for the duration of the contract. In more recent years provision has been made in such contracts for periodic inspection by State officials.
>
> (b) *The General Contract System*. Under this system all the prisoners are hired out to a single contractor, but, in contrast to the lease system, the State supplies the buildings and the necessary equipment for housing the prisoners and guards them. For the latter purpose the State appoints and pays officials. The contractor feeds the prisoners, provides the raw material and

tools, and pays the State a lump sum. In return the State hands over the prisoners' labour to the contractor.

(c) *The Special Contract System.* As under the general contract system, the State supplies the buildings and the necessary equipment for housing the prisoners but, in contrast to that system, the State retains the whole administration of the prisons. The prisoners, individually or in groups, are allotted to the contractor, the prison authorities selecting the prisoners in each case. The contractor supplies the raw material and tools and his agents direct the work, being admitted to the prison for this purpose. He pays for the prisoners' work at daily or piece rates. As in the other systems, the whole output belongs to the contractor.[54]

Placed at the disposal of. Arrangements where the private company is not paying the public authority as provider of the prisoner's services, but is on the contrary being subsidized by the State for the running of a private prison, indeed differ from what would normally be considered as hiring (or lease) arrangements. However, the position of a person placed by the State with the obligation to work in a prison run by a private contractor is not affected by the question of whether the contractor pays the State or the State subsidizes the contractor. For the purposes of the Convention, in the first case, the prisoner is "hired to" the private contractor; in the second, he or she is "placed at the disposal of" the latter.[55]

Role of private profit or benefit. The question of the direction in which payments flow between the State and private contractors leads to the issue of profit or benefit. Nothing suggests that the absence of balance sheet profit would negate the applicability to particular private entities of the provisions of the Convention prohibiting that a person be "hired to or placed at the disposal of private individuals, companies or associations".[56]

(iii) Conditions for private employment of prisoners

Compulsory prison labour is exempted from the scope of the Convention only where the labour is not hired to or placed at the disposal of private individuals, companies or associations.[57] In some countries, however, certain prisoners may, particularly during the period preceding their release, voluntarily accept employment with private employers, subject to guarantees as to the payment of normal wages and social security, consent of trade unions, etc.[58] The question thus arises as to whether prisoners, notwithstanding their captive circumstances, can be in a situation of truly voluntary labour, for which they have offered themselves voluntarily and without the menace of any penalty, including the loss of a right or advantage,[59] so that their work does not come under the definition of forced or compulsory labour given in Article 2, paragraph 1, of the Convention. If that is the case, the conditions laid down in Article 2, paragraph 2(c), for compulsory prison labour do not apply, and private employment of prisoners becomes possible.

In the first place, private employment of prison labour must depend on the formal consent of the prisoner concerned.[60] But the requirement of such

The abolition of forced or compulsory labour

formal consent is not in itself sufficient to eliminate the possibility that consent be given under the menace of loss of a right or advantage, or even of assignment to any compulsory work that can legally be imposed.[61] Prison labour is captive labour in the full sense of the term, namely, it has no access in law and in practice to employment other than under the conditions set unilaterally by the prison administration. Therefore, it seems difficult or even impossible, particularly in the prison context, to reconstitute the conditions of a free working relationship in the absence of an employment contract and outside the scope of the labour law.[62]

Conditions approximating a free labour relationship are the most reliable indicator of the voluntariness of labour. Such conditions would not have to emulate all the conditions which are applicable to a free market, but in the areas of wages, social security, safety and health, and labour inspection, the circumstances in which the prison labour is performed should not be so disproportionately lower than the free market that it could be characterized as exploitative. These facts will need to be weighed together with the circumstances under which formal consent has been given in order to ascertain whether the Convention is being respected when private entities are involved with prison labour.[63]

(d) Emergencies

The Convention exempts from its provisions "any work or service exacted in cases of emergency, that is to say, in the event of war or of a calamity or threatened calamity, such as fire, flood, famine, earthquake, violent epidemic or epizootic diseases, invasion by animal, insect or vegetable pests, and in general any circumstance that would endanger the existence or the well-being of the whole or part of the population".[64]

The concept of emergency – as indicated by the enumeration of examples in the Convention – involves a sudden, unforeseen happening calling for instant countermeasures. To respect the limits of the exception provided for in the Convention, the power to call up labour should be confined to genuine cases of emergency. Moreover, the extent of compulsory service, as well as the purpose for which it is used, should be limited to what is strictly required by the exigencies of the situation. In the same manner as Article 2, paragraph (2)(a), of the Convention exempts from its scope "work exacted in virtue of compulsory military service laws" only "for work of a purely military character",[65] Article 2, paragraph (2)(d), concerning emergencies is no blanket licence for imposing – on the occasion of war, fire or earthquake – any kind of compulsory service, but can only be invoked for service that is strictly required to counter an imminent danger to the population.[66]

(e) Minor communal services

The Convention also exempts from its provisions "minor communal services of a kind which, being performed by the members of the community in the direct interest of the said community, can therefore be considered as normal civic obligations incumbent upon the members of the community, provided that the members of the community or their direct representative shall have the right to be consulted in regard to the need for such services".[67] The ILO supervisory bodies[68] have drawn attention to the criteria which determine the limits of this exception and serve to distinguish it from other forms of compulsory services which, under the terms of the Convention, must be abolished (such as forced labour for general or local public works). These criteria are as follows:

- The services must be "minor services", i.e. relate primarily to maintenance work and – in exceptional cases – to the erection of certain buildings intended to improve the social conditions of the population of the community itself (a small school, a medical consultation and treatment room, etc.).[69]
- The services must be "communal services" performed "in the direct interest of the community", and not relate to the execution of works intended to benefit a wider group.
- The "members of the community" (i.e. the community which has to perform the services) or their "direct" representative (e.g. the village council) must "have the right to be consulted in regard to the need for such services".

4.2.4 Present status of Article 1, paragraph 2, and Articles 4 et seq. of the Convention

While States ratifying the Convention are obliged "to suppress the use of forced or compulsory labour in all its forms[70] within the shortest possible period",[71] the Convention, as adopted in 1930, provides that: "With a view to this complete suppression, recourse to forced or compulsory labour may be had during the transitional period, for public purposes only and as an exceptional measure, subject to the conditions and guarantees hereinafter provided."[72]

However, since the Convention, adopted in 1930, calls for the suppression of forced labour within the shortest possible period, to invoke at the current time that certain forms of forced or compulsory labour comply with one of the requirements of this set of provisions is to disregard the transitional function of these provisions and contradict the spirit of the Convention, as well as the status of the abolition of forced or compulsory labour in general international law as a peremptory norm from which no derogation is permitted.[73] Consequently, the ILO supervisory bodies have considered that the use of a form of forced or compulsory labour falling within the scope of the Convention as defined in Article 2 may no longer be justified by invoking observance of the provisions of Article 1, paragraph 2, and Articles 4-24, although the absolute prohibitions contained in these provisions remain binding upon the States having ratified the Convention.[74]

4.3 THE ABOLITION OF FORCED LABOUR CONVENTION, 1957 (NO. 105)

4.3.1 Substantive provisions

Under Article 2 of the Convention:

Each Member of the International Labour Organisation which ratifies this Convention undertakes to take effective measures to secure the immediate and complete abolition of forced or compulsory labour as specified in Article 1 of this Convention.

According to Article 1:

Each Member of the International Labour Organisation which ratifies this Convention undertakes to suppress and not to make use of any form of forced or compulsory labour:
(a) as a means of political coercion or education or as a punishment for holding or expressing political views or views ideologically opposed to the established political, social or economic system;
(b) as a means of mobilising and using labour for purposes of economic development;
(c) as a means of labour discipline;
(d) as a punishment for having participated in strikes;
(e) as a means of racial, social, national or religious discrimination.

Before addressing the specific circumstances referred to in the five cases enumerated in Article 1(a)-(e) of the Convention,[75] it is necessary to examine more generally the scope of Convention No. 105 against the background of Convention No. 29 and, in this connection, the definition of forced or compulsory labour and the role of the exceptions made from Convention No. 29, in particular as regards compulsory prison labour.

4.3.2 Scope of Convention No. 105 in relation to Convention No. 29 and compulsory prison labour

Convention No. 105 does not constitute a revision of Convention No. 29, but was designed to supplement the earlier instrument.[76] In the absence of a definition of "forced or compulsory labour" in Convention No. 105, the definition contained in the earlier Convention has been considered generally valid,[77] namely "all work or service which is exacted from any person under the menace of any penalty and for which the said person has not offered himself voluntarily".[78]

However, while Convention No. 29 calls for the general abolition of forced or compulsory labour in all its forms – subject to the exceptions set out in Article 2, paragraph 2[79] – Convention No. 105 requires the abolition of any form of forced or compulsory labour only in the five cases listed in Article 1 of that Convention.[80] Thus limited in scope by comparison with the general purview of the earlier instrument, Convention No. 105 accordingly covers new ground only because the exceptions from Convention No. 29 made in its Article 2, paragraph 2, "for the purposes of this Convention", and in particular the exemption concerning prison labour,[81] do not automatically apply to the later instrument, which was designed to supplement the 1930 Convention.[82]

Convention No. 105 does not prohibit the exaction of forced or compulsory labour from common offenders convicted, for example, of robbery, kidnapping, bombing or other acts of violence or acts or omissions that have endangered the life or health of others. Although a prisoner may be directed to work under the menace of a punishment and against his or her will, the labour in this instance is not imposed on him or her for one of the reasons cited in the Convention. Consequently, in most cases, labour imposed on persons as a consequence of a conviction in a court of law will have no relevance to the application of the Convention. On the other hand, if a person is in any way forced to work because he or she holds or has expressed particular political views, has committed a breach of labour discipline or has participated in a strike,[83] the situation is covered by the Convention, which prohibits the use "of any form" of forced or compulsory labour as a sanction, as a means of coercion, education or discipline, or as a punishment in respect of the persons within the ambit of Article 1(a), (c) and (d).[84]

In this connection, the supervisory bodies have noted that, while prison labour exacted from common offenders is intended to reform or rehabilitate them, the same need does not arise in the case of persons convicted for their opinions or for having taken part in a strike. Furthermore, in the case of persons convicted for expressing certain political views, an intention to reform or educate them through labour would in itself be covered by the express terms of the Convention, which applies, inter alia, to any form of compulsory labour as a means of political education.[85] For all these reasons, the ILO supervisory bodies have considered that compulsory labour in any form, including compulsory prison labour, is covered by Convention No. 105 when it is exacted in one of the five cases specified by that Convention.

Compliance of penal laws with the Convention can accordingly be ensured at different levels: at the level of civil and social rights and liberties when, in particular, political activities and the expression of political views, the manifestation of ideological opposition, breaches of labour discipline and the participation in strikes are beyond the purview of criminal punishment; at the level of the penalties that may be imposed, when these are limited to fines or other sanctions that do not involve an obligation to work; and, finally, at the level of the prison system: in a certain number of coun-

The abolition of forced or compulsory labour

tries, the law has traditionally conferred a special status on prisoners convicted of certain political offences, comparable to that conferred on persons in detention while awaiting trial, under which they are free from prison labour imposed on common offenders – although they may pursue an activity at their request.

4.3.3 Circumstances referred to in the Convention

(a) Political coercion
(Article 1(a) of the Convention)

Convention No. 105 prohibits the use of forced or compulsory labour as a means of political coercion or education or as a punishment for holding or expressing political views or views ideologically opposed to the established political, social or economic system. The range of activities which must be protected from punishment involving forced or compulsory labour thus comprises the freedom to express political or ideological views orally and through the press and other communications media, as well as various other generally recognized rights, such as the right of association and of assembly through which citizens seek to secure the dissemination and acceptance of their views and the adoption of policies and laws reflecting them, and which may be affected by measures of political coercion. Sanctions involving compulsory labour fall within the scope of the Convention where they enforce a prohibition of the expression of views or of opposition to the established political, social or economic system, whether such prohibition is imposed by law or by a discretionary administrative decision.[86]

However, certain limitations may be imposed by law on the rights and freedoms at stake "for the purpose of securing due recognition and respect for the rights and freedoms of others and of meeting the just requirements of morality, public order and the general welfare in a democratic society".[87] Thus, the Convention prohibits neither punishment by penalties involving compulsory labour of persons who use violence, incite to violence or engage in preparatory acts aimed at violence, nor judicial imposition of certain restrictions on persons convicted of crimes of this kind.[88]

In addition to the proper limits within which particular rights are to be exercised under normal circumstances, freedom of expression and other fundamental rights relevant to the Convention may during certain exceptional periods be subjected to temporary restrictions. The need for exceptional recourse to such measures is recognized in the International Covenant on Civil and Political Rights "[i]n time of public emergency which threatens the life of the nation and the existence of which is officially proclaimed"; in such cases, derogations from the provisions of the Covenant may be made "to the extent strictly required by the exigencies of the situation".[89] The ILO supervisory bodies have adopted a similar approach in regard to emergency measures, such as the suppression of fundamental rights and freedoms, which may have a bearing on the application of Article 1(a) of the Convention where the measures are enforced by sanctions involving compulsory labour. Recourse to such exceptional powers must be limited to what is necessary to meet circumstances that would endanger the life, personal safety or health of the whole or part of the population.[90]

(b) Economic development
(Article 1(b) of the Convention)

Article 1(b) of the Convention prohibits the use of forced or compulsory labour "as a method of mobilising and using labour for purposes of economic development". It follows from the terms "mobilising" and "economic development" used here that Article 1(b) is aimed at circumstances where recourse to forced or compulsory labour has a certain quantitative significance and is used for economic ends.[91] The prohibition applies even where recourse to forced labour as a method of mobilizing and using labour for purposes of economic development is of temporary or exceptional nature.[92]

(c) Labour discipline
(Article 1(c) of the Convention)

Forced or compulsory labour as a means of labour discipline may be of two kinds. It may consist of measures to ensure the due performance by a worker of his or her service under compulsion of law (in the form of physical constraint or the menace of a penalty), or of a sanction for breaches of labour discipline with penalties involving an obligation to perform work. In the latter case, the ILO supervisory bodies have, however, distinguished between penalties imposed to enforce labour discipline as such (and therefore falling within the scope of the Convention) and penalties which punish breaches of labour discipline that impair or are liable to endanger the operation of essential services,[93] or which are committed either in the exercise of functions that are essential to safety or in circumstances where life or health are in danger. Such actions or omissions do not come under the protection of the Convention. However, in such cases there must exist an effective danger, not mere inconvenience. Furthermore, the workers concerned must remain free to terminate their employment by reasonable notice.[94] The supervisory bodies have identified means of labour discipline falling under the Convention, particularly in certain laws governing the public sector or merchant shipping.[95]

(d) Participation in strikes
(Article 1(d) of the Convention)

The Convention prohibits recourse to sanctions involving any form of forced or compulsory labour "as a punishment for having participated in strikes". However, the ILO supervisory bodies have noted[96] that the Conference Committee which considered the draft Convention agreed that "in

The abolition of forced or compulsory labour

Table 4.1 Instruments on the abolition of forced or compulsory labour

Instruments	Number of ratifications (31 August 2002)	Status
Up-to-date instruments (Conventions whose ratification is encouraged and Recommendations to which member States are invited to give effect.)		
Forced Labour Convention, 1930 (No. 29)	161	**Fundamental Convention.**
Forced Labour (Indirect Compulsion) Recommendation, 1930 (No. 35)	–	This Recommendation is related to a fundamental Convention and is considered up to date.
Abolition of Forced Labour Convention, 1957 (No. 105)	158	**Fundamental Convention.**
Outdated instruments (Instruments that are no longer up to date; this category includes the Conventions that member States are no longer invited to ratify and the Recommendations whose implementation is no longer encouraged.)		
Forced Labour (Regulation) Recommendation, 1930 (No. 36)	–	The Governing Body has noted that Recommendation No. 36 is obsolete and has decided to propose to the Conference the withdrawal of this Recommendation.

certain circumstances penalties could be imposed for participation in illegal strikes and that these penalties might include normal prison labour",[97] and that in particular such penalties might be imposed where there were "national laws prohibiting strikes in certain sectors or during conciliation proceedings" or where "trade unions voluntarily agreed to renounce the right to strike in certain circumstances".[98] In examining the compatibility of national laws on strikes with the Convention – in so far as they are enforceable with sanctions that may involve compulsory labour – the ILO supervisory bodies have followed the principles developed in the field of freedom of association[99] in ascertaining the specific limits to the right to strike, and in particular the restrictions concerning essential services and persons representing public authority, as well as those concerning emergency situations, political strikes and the conditions under which a strike may be called, so as to clarify the scope of the protection afforded by Article 1(d) of the Convention.[100]

(e) Discrimination
(Article 1(e) of the Convention)

Article 1(e) of the Convention prohibits the use of any form of compulsory labour "as a means of racial, social, national or religious discrimination". This provision requires the abolition of any discriminatory distinctions made on racial, social, national or religious grounds in exacting labour for the purpose of production or service, even where the labour

Fundamental rights at work and international labour standards

is not otherwise covered by the Conventions on forced labour[101] (for example, in the context of minor communal services).[102] Similarly, where punishment involving compulsory labour is meted out more severely to certain groups defined in racial, social, national or religious terms, this falls within the scope of the Convention,[103] even where the offence giving rise to the punishment is a common offence which does not otherwise come under the protection of Article 1(a), (c) or (d) of the Convention.

Notes

[1] Article 1, paragraph 1, of the Convention.

[2] For the definition of forced or compulsory labour given in the Convention and the exceptions from its scope, see subsections 4.2.2 and 4.2.3 below.

[3] Article 25 of the Convention.

[4] Article 2, paragraph 1, of the Convention.

[5] Article 2, paragraph 2, of the Convention – see subsection 4.2.3. below.

[6] In the text of the Convention, the criterion of not having offered oneself voluntarily is distinct from that of "the menace of any penalty". However, where consent to work or service already was given "under the menace of a penalty", the two criteria overlap: there is no "voluntary offer" under threat. But the distinction between the two criteria becomes meaningful where there is a difference in time, as in the text of the Convention: a person may have volunteered for a career in the armed forces and thereby freely and knowingly accepted a position where desertion becomes punishable.

[7] ILO: *Abolition of forced labour*, General Survey of the Reports relating to the Forced Labour Convention, 1930 (No. 29), and the Abolition of Forced Labour Convention, 1957 (No. 105), Report of the Committee of Experts on the Application of Conventions and Recommendations, Report III (Part 4B), ILC, 65th Session, 1979 (hereinafter ILO: *Abolition of forced labour*, General Survey of 1979 by the Committee of Experts), para. 20.

[8] Universal Declaration of Human Rights, article 26; International Covenant on Economic, Social and Cultural Rights, articles 13 and 14.

[9] Provisions concerning the prescription of a school-leaving age appear, inter alia, in Article 15, paragraph 2, of the Social Policy (Basic Aims and Standards) Convention, 1962 (No. 117).

[10] In particular, the Special Youth Schemes Recommendation, 1970 (No. 136), indicates (Paragraph 7(1) and (2)(a)) that schemes of education and training involving obligatory enrolment of unemployed young people are compatible with the Conventions on forced labour, but requires prior consent for any schemes involving an obligation to serve (Paragraph 7(1) and (2)(b)).

[11] ILO: *Abolition of forced labour*, General Survey of 1979 by the Committee of Experts, para. 20, referring also to earlier sources.

[12] ibid.

[13] ILO: *Record of Proceedings*, ILC, 14th Session, Geneva, 1930, Vol. I, p. 691; ILO: *Abolition of forced labour*, General Survey of 1979 by the Committee of Experts, para. 21.

[14] Committee of Experts, direct request, 1999, Convention No. 29, United Kingdom.

[15] ILO: *Report of the Committee of Experts on the Application of Conventions and Recommendations*, Report III (Part 1A), ILC, 89th Session, 2001, General Report, para. 129; ibid., Report III (Part 4A), ILC, 82nd Session, 1995, observation, Convention No. 29, France.

[16] ILO: *Abolition of forced labour*, General Survey of 1979 by the Committee of Experts, paras. 97-101.

The abolition of forced or compulsory labour

[17] For example, report of the Commission of Inquiry appointed under article 26 of the Constitution of the International Labour Organization to examine the observance of certain international labour Conventions by the Dominican Republic and Haiti with respect to the employment of Haitian workers on the sugar plantations of the Dominican Republic (ILO: *Official Bulletin*, Special Supplement, Vol. LXVI, 1983, Series B); report of the Committee set up to examine the representation made by the CLAT under article 24 of the ILO Constitution alleging non-observance by Brazil of the Forced Labour Convention, 1930 (No. 29), and the Abolition of Forced Labour Convention, 1957 (No. 105).

[18] ILO: *Abolition of forced labour*, General Survey of 1979 by the Committee of Experts, para. 45.

[19] See below subsections 4.2.3(a) and 4.2.3(c).

[20] ibid.

[21] See also the United Nations Convention against Transnational Organized Crime and the Protocol supplementing it to Prevent, Suppress and Punish Trafficking in Persons, Especially Women and Children (United Nations doc. A/55/383 and Add.1); article 3, subparagraph (b), of the Protocol specifies that "The consent of a victim of trafficking in persons to the intended exploitation set forth in subparagraph (a) of this article shall be irrelevant where any of the means [of coercion, fraud, deception, abuse of power, etc.] set forth in subparagraph (a) have been used."

[22] See subsection 4.2.1 above.

[23] ILO: *Report of the Committee of Experts ...*, Report III (Part 4A), ILC, 70th Session, 1984, observation, Convention No. 29, Federal Republic of Germany.

[24] ILO: Governing Body, Nov. 1997, doc. GB.270/15/3, para. 30.

[25] ILO: *Report of the Committee of Experts ...*, Report III (Part 4A), ILC, 83rd Session, 1996, observation, Convention No. 29, Pakistan, para. 5; Report of the Commission of Inquiry appointed under article 26 of the Constitution of the International Labour Organization to examine the observance by Myanmar of the Forced Labour Convention, 1930 (No. 29) (ILO, *Official Bulletin*, Special Supplement, Vol. LXXXI, 1998, Series B, p. 59, para. 206).

[26] For example, the Minimum Age Convention, 1973 (No. 138), Article 3, paragraph 1, and the Worst Forms of Child Labour Convention, 1999 (No. 182), Articles 1, 2 and 3, paragraph (d).

[27] Also, under article 3, subparagraph (c), of the Protocol to Prevent, Suppress and Punish Trafficking in Persons, Especially Women and Children, already referred to in note 21 above, "The recruitment, transportation, transfer, harbouring or receipt of a child for the purpose of exploitation shall be considered 'trafficking in persons', even if this does not involve any of the means [of coercion, etc.] set forth in subparagraph (a) of this article"; subparagraph (d) specifies that "child" shall mean any person under 18 years of age.

[28] For example, ILO: *Report of the Committee of Experts ...*, Report III (Part 1A), ILC, 89th Session, 2001, observations, Convention No. 29, Haiti, India, Indonesia, Sri Lanka, Thailand.

[29] ILO: *Abolition of forced labour*, General Survey of 1979 by the Committee of Experts, para. 71; ILO: *Report of the Committee of Experts ...*, Report III (Part 4A), ILC, 68th Session, 1982, observation, Convention No. 29, Belgium.

[30] ILO: *Abolition of forced labour*, General Survey of 1979 by the Committee of Experts, para. 68. The Committee of Experts also noted, as an illustration of this principle, that Article 1(a) of the Supplementary Convention of 1956 on the abolition of slavery, the slave trade, and institutions and practices similar to slavery refers, inter alia, to the status or condition arising from a pledge by a debtor of his personal services if the length and nature of those services are not respectively limited and defined.

[31] (In peacetime.) However, where previous acceptance to serve a number of years was given in exchange for higher education received, e.g. to become a physician or a pilot, a differentiated approach is called for, taking into account such elements as the proportionality

of obligations, the possibility of reimbursing the cost of studies, the penalties that may be imposed, etc. – see ILO: *Abolition of forced labour*, General Survey of 1979 by the Committee of Experts, paras. 72 and 60.

[32] See, for example, ILO: *Report of the Committee of Experts ...*, Report III (Part 1A), ILC, 88th Session, 2000, observation, Convention No. 29, Pakistan; ibid., Report III (Part 1A), ILC, 87th Session, 1999, observation, Convention No. 29, Bangladesh.

[33] ILO: *Report of the Committee of Experts ...*, Report III (Part 1A), ILC, 89th Session, 2001, observation, Convention No. 29, Iraq.

[34] Legislation repealed in 1998 – ILO: *Report of the Committee of Experts ...*, op. cit., 1999, observation, Convention No. 29, Netherlands.

[35] Article 2, para. 2(a).

[36] ILO: *Abolition of forced labour*, General Survey of 1979 by the Committee of Experts, para. 24, with references to the preparatory work of Convention No. 29.

[37] See subsections 4.3.1 and 4.3.3(b) below. The ILC reasserted this principle when discussing the draft Special Youth Schemes Recommendation, 1970 (No. 136); the Conference heeded the incompatibility with the forced labour Conventions of a proposal under which young people could have been obliged to take part in special employment schemes directed to national development, provided they were undertaken within the framework of compulsory military service or as an alternative to such service – see ILO: *Abolition of forced labour*, General Survey of 1979 by the Committee of Experts, para. 25, with references to the preparatory work of Recommendation No. 136.

[38] ILO: ibid., paras. 26-32.

[39] Article 2, paragraph 2(d), of the Convention – see subsection (d) below.

[40] ILO: *Abolition of forced labour*, General Survey of 1979 by the Committee of Experts, para. 31.

[41] Article 2, paragraph 2(b), of the Convention.

[42] ILO: *Abolition of forced labour*, General Survey of 1979 by the Committee of Experts, para. 34.

[43] See subsection (a) above.

[44] Article 2, paragraph 2(d), of the Convention. See subsection (d) below.

[45] Article 2, paragraph 2(e), of the Convention. See subsection (e) below.

[46] ILO: *Abolition of forced labour*, General Survey of 1979 by the Committee of Experts, para. 34.

[47] Article 2, paragraph 2(c), of the Convention.

[48] ILO: *Abolition of forced labour*, General Survey of 1979 by the Committee of Experts, para. 90.

[49] ibid., para. 94.

[50] In adopting this provision, the Conference expressly rejected an amendment which would have permitted the hiring of prison labour to private undertakings engaged in the execution of public works (ILO: *Record of Proceedings*, ILC, 14th Session, Geneva, 1930, pp. 305-308).

[51] ILO: *Report of the Committee of Experts ...*, Report III (Part 1A), ILC, 89th Session, 2001, General Report, paras. 86 and 119.

[52] ILO: *Report of the Committee of Experts ...*, Report III (Part 1A), ILC, 86th Session, 1998, General Report, para. 124.

[53] The essential parts of the Memorandum were published under the title "prison labour", in *International Labour Review*, Vol. XXV, No. 3 (Mar. 1932), pp. 311-331, and No. 4 (Apr. 1932), pp. 499-524.

[54] ILO: *Report of the Committee of Experts ...*, 2001, op. cit., General Report, paras. 96 and 122. The Committee of Experts further notes in paras. 97 and 98 that in its 1931 Memorandum the Office notes that "it has not yet been possible to eradicate the lease system

The abolition of forced or compulsory labour

entirely", despite its drawbacks, because "the system offers considerable financial advantages to the State", and that the general contract system "is now practically a matter of history. The special contract system on the contrary, is still common in prison labour".

[55] ibid., para. 123.

[56] ibid., paras. 124-127. The Committee of Experts notes, inter alia, from the preparatory work that the amendment which introduced to Article 2(2)(c) the words "or placed at the disposal of", following a proposal of the Workers' group, "intended to strengthen the clause", and also added the words "companies or other entities". The words "other entities", subsequently replaced by "associations", would also cover non-profit-making associations.

[57] See subsection 4.2.3(c)(ii) above on conditions governing the use of compulsory prison labour.

[58] ILO: *Abolition of forced labour*, General Survey of 1979 by the Committee of Experts, para. 97.

[59] See subsections 4.2.2(b) and 4.2.2(c) above, and ILO: *Report of the Committee of Experts* ..., 2001, op. cit., General Report, paras. 128 et seq.

[60] ILO: *Abolition of forced labour*, General Survey of 1979 by the Committee of Experts, paras. 97, et seq.; see also subsection 4.2.2(c)(i), above, "Form and subject matter of consent".

[61] ILO: *Report of the Committee of Experts* ..., 2001, op. cit., General Report, paras. 129-130; see also subsections 4.2.2(b) and (c) above.

[62] ILO: *Report of the Committee of Experts* ..., 2001, op. cit., General Report, para. 130.

[63] ibid., para. 143. See also, with regard to arm's length conditions of employment, ILO: *Report of the Committee of Experts* ..., Report III (Part 1A), ILC, 90th Session, 2002, Convention No. 29, general observation, paras. 10 and 11, and observations on Australia, Austria and the United Kingdom.

[64] Article 2, paragraph 2(d), of the Convention.

[65] See subsection 4.2.3(c) above.

[66] ILO: *Abolition of forced labour*, General Survey of 1979 by the Committee of Experts, para. 36; idem: *Report of the Committee of Experts* ..., 1997, observation, Convention No. 29, Japan.

[67] Article 2, paragraph 2(e), of the Convention.

[68] ILO: *Abolition of forced labour*, General Survey of 1979 of the Committee of Experts, para. 37; Report of the Committee of Inquiry appointed under article 26 of the Constitution of the International Labour Organization to examine the observance by Myanmar of the Forced Labour Convention, 1930 (No. 29) (*Official Bulletin* (Geneva, ILO), Special Supplement, Vol. LXXXI, 1998, Series B, para. 213).

[69] Since even the public works of general interest that come under the definition of forced labour, but were tolerated during a transitional period (see subsection 4.2.4), were not only strictly regulated but also restricted to a maximum of 60 days per year (Article 12 of the Convention), the minor nature of "minor services" entirely exempted from the very definition of forced labour is to be reflected in a duration of an incomparably smaller magnitude.

[70] Other than those specifically excluded from the scope of the Convention (see subsection 4.2.3 above).

[71] Article 1, paragraph 1, of the Convention.

[72] Article 2, paragraph 2, of the Convention.

[73] Report of the Commission of Inquiry appointed under article 26 of the Constitution of the International Labour Organization to examine the observance by Myanmar of the Forced Labour Convention, 1930 (No. 29) (*Official Bulletin*, Special Supplement, Vol. LXXXI, 1998, Series B), para. 218; ILO: *Report of the Committee of Experts* ..., 1998, op. cit., observation, Convention No. 29, Bangladesh; ILO: *Report of the Committee of the Experts* ..., 2000, op. cit., observation, Convention No. 29, Myanmar.

[74] ibid.

Fundamental rights at work and international labour standards

[75] See subsection 4.3.3 below.

[76] ILO: *Abolition of forced labour*, General Survey of 1979 by the Committee of Experts, paras. 9 and 104.

[77] ibid., para. 39.

[78] Convention No. 29, Article 2, paragraph 1 – see subsection 4.2.2 above.

[79] See subsections 4.2.1 and 4.2.3 above.

[80] See subsection 4.3.1 above.

[81] See subsection 4.2.3(c) above.

[82] ILO: *Abolition of forced labour*, General Survey of 1979 by the Committee of Experts, para. 104. The Committee of Experts recalls in this connection that the Convention was adopted following a survey by the UN-ILO Ad Hoc Committee on Forced Labour, which found that one of the most common forms of forced labour in the world was forced labour as a means of political coercion. Many of the specific cases from which the Ad Hoc Committee drew this conclusion related to labour resulting from penal legislation, involving conviction by a court of law. The Governing Body of the ILO accordingly decided to include an item on forced labour in the agenda of the Conference and expressed the view that any subsequent instrument adopted by the Conference should deal with the practices which are specifically excluded from the scope of the 1930 Convention (ibid., footnote, with references to the preparatory work).

[83] The scope of the Convention as regards certain restrictions relating specifically to freedom of opinion and the right to strike is examined in subsections 4.3.3(a) and (d) below.

[84] ILO: *Abolition of forced labour*, General Survey of 1979 by the Committee of Experts, paras. 105 and 106.

[85] ibid., para. 108. The point had already been made in the course of the preparatory work on the Convention that, in most countries, it is regarded as normal that persons convicted of certain categories of crime should be required to work during the period of their sentence, that such work serves an educational purpose and helps keep up the morale of prisoners and that it may be felt that it is reasonable to permit this type of forced labour and undesirable to attempt to forbid it in any way. However, it was pointed out in the preparatory report submitted to the Conference that this same form of forced labour can lead to abuses, particularly if persons may be sentenced to penal labour on account of their political or other beliefs. The proposed instrument should guard against this (ILO: *Abolition of forced labour*, General Survey of 1979 of the Committee of Experts, para. 107, with references to the preparatory work).

[86] ILO: *Abolition of forced labour*, General Survey of 1979 by the Committee of Experts, para. 133.

[87] Universal Declaration of Human Rights, 1948, article 29; see also articles 5, 21 and 22 of the International Covenant on Civil and Political Rights, 1966.

[88] ILO: *Abolition of forced labour*, General Survey of 1979 of the Committee of Experts, para. 133.

[89] Article 4 of the International Covenant on Civil and Political Rights, 1966.

[90] ILO: *Abolition of forced labour*, General Survey of 1979 by the Committee of Experts, para. 134. The criteria for an emergency and the requirement of proportionality of the measures taken correspond to what has been stated in subsection 3.1.3(d) with regard to Article 2, paragraph 2(d), of Convention No. 29, concerning work or service exacted in cases of emergency. See also subsection (d) below regarding exceptional prohibitions of strikes.

[91] ILO: *Abolition of forced labour*, General Survey of 1979 of the Committee of Experts, para. 40.

[92] The Conference declined to limit the prohibition in Article 1(b) to the use of forced labour as a "normal" method of mobilizing and using labour for purposes of economic development (ILO: *Record of Proceedings*, ILC, 39th Session, Geneva, 1956, p. 723, para. 11; ibid., 40th Session, Geneva, 1957, p. 709, para. 11).

The abolition of forced or compulsory labour

[93] That is, services, the interruption of which may endanger the life, personal safety or health of the whole or part of the population; this criterion corresponds to what has been stated above (for emergency situations, see subsection (a) and note 90 above).

[94] ILO: *Abolition of forced labour*, General Survey of 1979 by the Committee of Experts, para. 110.

[95] See, inter alia, ibid., paras. 111-119; and Committee of Experts, various more recent comments on the observance of the Convention in a number of countries.

[96] ILO: *Abolition of forced labour*, General Survey of 1979 by the Committee of Experts, para. 120.

[97] ILO: *Record of Proceedings*, ILC, 40th Session, Geneva, 1957, p. 709, para. 14.

[98] idem, 39th Session, Geneva, 1956, p. 723, para. 12.

[99] See Chapter 2.

[100] See also ILO: *Abolition of forced labour*, General Survey of 1979 of the Committee of Experts, paras. 122-132.

[101] ibid., para. 42.

[102] See subsection 4.2.3(e) above (and subsection 4.3.3(b) as regards the quantitative significance of what comes under Article 1(b) of Convention No. 105).

[103] ILO: *Abolition of forced labour*, General Survey of 1979 of the Committee of Experts, para. 141.

EQUALITY OF OPPORTUNITY AND TREATMENT IN EMPLOYMENT AND OCCUPATION

5

Constance THOMAS and Yuki HORII

5.1 INTRODUCTION

Since the International Labour Organization was founded in 1919, the question of the observance of equality of opportunity and treatment has been one of its fundamental objectives. The original Constitution of the ILO indicated that this principle is among those that are "of special interest and urgent importance" and that the "standards set by law in each country with respect to the economic conditions should have due regard to the equitable economic treatment of all workers lawfully resident therein". The original Constitution further recognized "the principle of equal work for work of equal value".[1] In a resolution adopted in 1938, the International Labour Conference invited all Members "to apply the principle of equality of treatment to all workers resident in their territory, and to renounce all measures of exception which might in particular establish discrimination against workers belonging to certain races or confessions with regard to their admission to public or private posts".[2]

The Declaration of Philadelphia affirms that "all human beings, irrespective of race, creed or sex, have the right to pursue both their material well-being and their spiritual development in conditions of freedom and dignity, of economic security and equal opportunity". It further proclaims that the attainment of the conditions making it possible to achieve equality of opportunity and treatment shall be the central aim of national and international policy, and that "all national and international policies and measures, in particular those of an economic and financial character, should be judged in this light and accepted only in so far as they may be held to promote and not to hinder the achievement of this fundamental objective".[3]

The first binding international instruments to be adopted with the specific objective of promoting equality and eliminating discrimination were the Equal Remuneration Convention, 1951 (No. 100), and its accompanying Recommendation (No. 90). These instruments were limited to the promotion of equality between men and women and the issue of pay. Upon their adoption, it was recognized that equal pay could not be achieved without the elimination of discrimination in all areas of employment and that other grounds of discrimination should also be the subjects of prohibition. Thus, these instruments were shortly followed, in 1958, with the adoption by the International Labour Conference of the Discrimination (Employment and Occupation) Convention (No. 111), and Recommendation (No. 111), which address all forms of discrimination concerning employment and occupation. They cover all workers and prohibit discrimination on seven grounds (race, colour, sex, religion, political opinion, national extraction and social origin).

Prior to the adoption of these instruments on equality, international labour standards directed specifically at women had been aimed at providing protection through prohibition, restriction or special measures. A marked shift in emphasis from special protection to the promotion of equality in the standard-setting activities of the ILO regarding women occurred during 1975, when the International Labour Conference adopted a Declaration on Equality of Opportunity and Treatment for Women Workers.[4] The Declaration recalls that the protection of women at work should be an integral part of the efforts aimed at continuous promotion and improvement of living and working conditions of all employees. It provides that women should be protected "on the same basis and with the same standards of protection as men"; that studies and research should be undertaken and measures taken to protect against processes which might have a harmful effect on women and men from the standpoint of their social function of reproduction. In 1985 the International Labour Conference adopted a resolution on equal opportunities and equal treatment for men and women in employment.[5] With respect to the issue of protective measures, the resolution recommends that all protective legislation applying to women should be reviewed in the light of up-to-date scientific knowledge and technical changes and that it should be revised, supplemented, extended, retained or repealed, according to national circumstances. The Committee of Experts on the Application of Conventions and Recommendations, in its General Survey on night work of women in industry, 2001,[6] recently affirmed this approach and confirmed that protection and equality have and should guide standard-setting action in matters of women's employment.

In 1975, the International Labour Conference, based on the new approach that equality can only be achieved by improving the general conditions of work of all workers, both women and men, invited the Governing Body to include the issue of workers with family responsibilities on the agenda of the earliest possible session of the Conference with a view to the adoption of a new instrument. During the General Discussion at the Conference, it was pointed out that any change in the traditional role of women would have to be accompanied by a change in that of men, greater sharing in family life and household tasks, and equal access for men and women to all services and arrangements made in these fields.

Equality of opportunity and treatment

The Employment (Women with Family Responsibilities) Recommendation (No. 123), which had been adopted in 1965 to provide measures that should be taken to allow women to harmonize their various responsibilities without being exposed to discrimination, was considered to be out of date as it did not question placing the burden of responsibility for such matters solely on women, but sought to alleviate some of the hardship these dual and seemingly competing responsibilities caused.

In this context, the Governing Body decided to include in the 66th Session (1980) of the International Labour Conference the question of equality of opportunity and treatment for workers of both sexes having family responsibilities. In 1981, the International Labour Conference adopted the Workers with Family Responsibilities Convention, 1981 (No. 156), and its accompanying Recommendation (No. 165).

In addition to the general standards on non-discrimination and equality, other international labour standards address the issue of non-discrimination or promotion of equality as either their main objective or as a specific provision. These instruments serve to emphasize that in certain domains particular attention needs to be drawn to the promotion of equality among members of particular groups. For example, the Social Policy (Basic Aims and Standards) Convention, 1962 (No. 117), provides that the aim of any social policy shall be to eliminate all discrimination among workers on grounds of race, colour, sex, belief, tribal association or trade union affiliation. The Employment Policy Convention, 1964 (No. 122), states that employment policy shall aim at ensuring that there is freedom of choice of employment and the fullest possible opportunity for each worker to qualify for, and to use skills and endowments in, a job for which he or she is well suited, irrespective of race, colour, sex, religion, political opinion, national extraction or social origin. More specifically, Article 8 of the Paid Educational Leave Convention, 1974 (No. 140), prohibits the denial of such leave on the grounds of race, colour, sex, religion, political opinion, national extraction or social origin. Article 5 of the Termination of Employment Convention, 1982 (No. 158), includes race, colour, sex, marital status, family responsibilities, pregnancy, religion, political opinion, national extraction, social origin, maternity leave and union membership or participation as invalid reasons for termination. In some instances, Convention No. 111 is specially referred to in other Conventions. For example, the Rural Workers' Organisations Convention, 1975 (No. 141), provides in Article 4 for the development of strong and independent organizations of rural workers "as an effective means of ensuring the participation of rural workers, without discrimination, as defined in the Discrimination (Employment and Occupation) Convention, 1958 ...".

Other standards that address specific groups of workers who are often the subject of discriminatory treatment, and that promote equality, among other measures, for such groups, include the international labour standards concerning migrant workers, indigenous and tribal peoples, workers with disabilities and older workers.

Fundamental rights at work and international labour standards

The elimination of discrimination was reaffirmed as a principle inherent in any ILO policy by the adoption in 1998 of the ILO Declaration on Fundamental Principles and Rights at Work and its Follow-up. The Declaration states that the fundamental rights of workers, which are clearly set out in four principles, including the elimination of discrimination in respect of employment and occupation, are so essential to the mandate of the ILO that membership of the Organization by a State in itself creates an obligation to promote these rights, even if the State has not ratified the fundamental Conventions which set forth these four principles. The Declaration refers to the principles contained in Conventions Nos. 100 and 111, the two fundamental Conventions in relation to non-discrimination.

In 1995, the Director-General of the ILO launched a campaign for the ratification of the fundamental Conventions. The above Conventions are among the most widely ratified of the international labour Conventions.

A summary of the relevant ILO instruments is given in table 5.1 on p. 84.

5.2 CONTENT OF THE STANDARDS ON NON-DISCRIMINATION

5.2.1 Discrimination in employment and occupation: The Discrimination (Employment and Occupation) Convention (No. 111), and Recommendation (No. 111), 1958

(a) Scope of the instruments as regards individuals, definition and grounds of discrimination[7]

(i) Scope of the instruments as regards individuals

No provision of the Convention or the Recommendation limits their scope as regards individuals and occupations. The elimination of discrimination in employment and occupation therefore applies to all workers, both nationals and non-nationals.[8] They therefore apply to workers in both the public and the private sectors.

(ii) Definition of discrimination[9]

Article 1, paragraph 1(a), of the Convention defines discrimination as "any distinction, exclusion or preference [made on certain grounds], which has the effect of nullifying or impairing equality of opportunity or treatment in employment or occupation".

This definition contains three elements: a factual element (the existence of a distinction, exclusion or preference which constitutes a difference in treatment); a criterion on which the difference in treatment is based; and the objective result of this difference in treatment, namely the nullification or impairment of equality of opportunity or treatment.

Through this broad definition, the Convention covers all discrimination that may affect equality of opportunity and treatment. The distinctions, exclusions or preferences covered under the Convention may have their origin in law or in practice.

In referring to the "effect" of a distinction, exclusion or preference on equality of opportunity and treatment, the definition uses the objective consequences of these measures as a criterion. Thus the Convention covers direct discrimination, such as expressly stated exclusions of persons who need not apply for jobs; and indirect forms of discrimination such as occupational segregation based on sex.

Indirect discrimination refers to apparently neutral situations, regulations, or practices, which in fact result in unequal treatment of persons with certain characteristics. It occurs when the same condition, treatment or criterion is applied to everyone, but results in a disproportionably harsh impact on some persons on the basis of certain characteristics or who belong to certain classes with specific characteristics such as race, sex or religion, and is not closely related to the inherent requirement of the job.

Intent is not an element of the definition under the Convention. The Convention covers all discrimination without referring to the intention of the author of a discriminatory act or even without there needing to be an identifiable author, such as in the case of indirect discrimination or occupational segregation.

(iii) Grounds of discrimination[10]

Grounds of discrimination referred to in Article 1, paragraph 1(a), of the Convention

These consist of a restrictive list of seven grounds of discrimination:

Race and colour. These grounds are generally examined together since difference of colour is only one, albeit the most apparent, of the ethnic characteristics that differentiate human beings. However, they are not considered to be identical as colour differences may exist between people of the same race. Under the Convention, the term "race" is often considered in a wide sense to refer to linguistic communities or minorities whose identity is based on religious or cultural characteristics, or even national extraction. Generally speaking, any discrimination against an ethnic group, including indigenous and tribal peoples, is considered to be racial discrimination within the terms of the Convention.

National extraction. The term "national extraction" in the Convention is not aimed at the distinctions that may be made between the citizens of the country concerned and those of another country, but covers distinctions made on the basis of a person's place of birth, ancestry or foreign origin. Distinctions made between citizens of the same country on the basis of the foreign birth or origins of some of them are one of the most evident examples. Thus it may be understood that discrimination based on national extraction means that action which may be directed against persons who are nationals of the country in question, but who have acquired their citizenship by naturalization or who are descendants of foreign immigrants, or persons belonging to groups of different national extraction or origin living in the same State.[11]

Sex. These are distinctions that are made explicitly or implicitly to the detriment of one sex or the other. While in the great majority of cases, and particularly in cases of indirect discrimination, they are detrimental to women, protection against discrimination applies equally to either sex. Discrimination on grounds of sex also includes discrimination based on: civil status; marital status, or more specifically family situation (particularly as regards responsibilities for dependent persons); pregnancy and confinement. These distinctions are not discriminatory *in themselves*, and only become so when they have the effect of imposing a requirement or condition on an individual of a particular sex that would not be imposed on an individual of the other sex. Distinctions based on pregnancy and confinement are discriminatory because they can only, by definition, affect women. "Sexual harassment" or "unsolicited sexual attention" are particular forms of discrimination on the basis of sex which have received increased attention.[12]

Religion. The Convention protects against discrimination based on denomination or faith, whether it is because of not being of a particular faith, or because of having a belief in a particular faith, or having no belief. It not only protects against discrimination based on belief in a religion, but also protects the expression and manifestation of the religion.

Social origin. This criterion refers to situations in which an individual's membership of a class, socio-occupational category or caste determines his or her occupational future, either because he or she is denied access to certain jobs or activities, or because he or she is only assigned certain jobs. Even in societies with considerable social mobility, a number of obstacles continue to prevent perfect equality of opportunity for the various social categories.[13]

Political opinion. This protection against discrimination on the basis of political opinion implies protection in respect of the activities of expressing or demonstrating opposition to established political principles and opinions. It may also cover discrimination based on political affiliation.

Other grounds of discrimination in Article 1, paragraph 1(b), of the Convention

These consist of "such other distinction, exclusion or preference which has the effect of nullifying or impairing equality of opportunity or treatment [...] as may be determined by the Member concerned after consultation with representative employers' and workers' organisations, where such exist, and with other appropriate bodies". The procedure for the implementation of this Article is not specified. However, in a large number of countries, governments are reporting on criteria of discrimination other than those set forth in Article 1, paragraph 1(a), of the Convention which have

Equality of opportunity and treatment

been incorporated in the Constitution, or in laws or regulations for the elimination of discrimination in employment and occupation. Two Conventions adopted after Convention No. 111 cover two of the criteria most frequently encountered at the national level. These are the Workers with Family Responsibilities Convention, 1981 (No. 156), and the Vocational Rehabilitation and Employment (Disabled Persons) Convention, 1983 (No. 159). Other criteria frequently encountered are state of health (including HIV-positive status), age, sexual orientation and membership or non-membership of a trade union.

(b) Substantive field of application of the Convention: Access to training, to occupation and employment, and terms and conditions of employment[14]

Article 1, paragraph 3, provides that the terms "employment" and "occupation" include access to vocational training, access to employment and to particular occupations, and terms and conditions of employment. The protection afforded by the Convention is not limited to individuals who have already gained access to employment or to an occupation, but also covers opportunities of gaining access to employment or to an occupation. It also covers access to training, without which there would be no real opportunity of access to employment or occupation. The Recommendation contains provisions illustrating these concepts more specifically (Paragraph 2(b)):

> (b) all persons should, without discrimination, enjoy equality of opportunity and treatment in respect of –
> (i) access to vocational guidance and placement services;
> (ii) access to training and employment of their own choice on the basis of individual suitability for such training or employment;
> (iii) advancement in accordance with their individual character, experience, ability and diligence;
> (iv) security of tenure of employment;
> (v) remuneration for work of equal value;
> (vi) conditions of work including hours of work, rest periods, annual holidays with pay, occupational safety and occupational health measures, as well as social security measures and welfare facilities and benefits provided in connection with employment.

Under Paragraph 2(d) of the Recommendation, employers should not practise or countenance discrimination "in engaging or training any person for employment, in advancing or retaining such person in employment, or in fixing terms and conditions of employment".

(i) Access to training and vocational guidance[15]

Training is of paramount importance in determining the actual opportunities for gaining access to employment and occupation, since discrimination at this stage will subsequently be perpetuated and aggravated in employment and in occupation. This term should not be interpreted in a narrow sense and should cover both apprenticeship and technical education, and general education, as well as "on the job" training.

Vocational guidance is intended to offer young persons or persons who may need it special assistance in choosing an occupation. A number of methods are used, such as the dissemination of information on occupations, the preparation of recommendations in the light of personal aptitudes and interests and social needs, and the joint participation of teachers and parents in fostering the choice of an occupation by children. It plays an important role in opening up a broad range of occupations, free of considerations based on stereotypes or archaic conceptions that specific trades or occupations are supposedly reserved for persons of a particular sex, ethnic group, or caste.

(ii) Access to employment and to various occupations[16]

The protection afforded by the Convention covers access to *wage-earning employment*, as well as self-employment. The term "occupation" means the trade, profession or type of work performed by an individual, irrespective of the branch of economic activity to which he or she belongs or his or her professional status. The two terms therefore have a very broad meaning.

Access to self-employed occupation. This category covers the majority of the active population in certain developing countries, and principally in the rural sector. It therefore includes various occupations and is of a heterogeneous nature. Access to the various material goods and services required to carry on the occupation therefore constitutes one of the objectives of the national policy to promote equality of opportunity and treatment in employment and occupation.

Placement. The existence of a public employment service may be an essential element of a policy to promote equality of opportunity and treatment in employment. Public and private employment agencies should be covered under the Convention in relation to their consideration and placement of candidates.

Access to wage-earning or salaried employment. This means that every individual has the right to have his or her application for appointment to the post of their choice considered equitably, without discrimination based on any of the grounds referred to in the Convention. The recruitment procedure and the statement of reasons in the event of an adverse decision on the application for appointment are of great importance for the respect of this right.

Access to the public service. The State, as an employer, is subject directly to the principles which it must promote and, in view of the volume of employment provided by the State, the public sector plays a key role in the general implementation of government policy to promote equality of opportunity and treatment in employment and occupation. Government agencies are not to discriminate in connection with employment.

Equality of opportunity and treatment

Access to employers' and workers' organizations. Paragraph 2(f) of Recommendation No. 111 provides that "employers' and workers' organisations should not practise or countenance discrimination in respect of admission, retention of membership or participation in their affairs". This provision concerns both the practices of employers' and workers' organizations as influenced by the provisions of national legislation or as determined by their own regulations.

(iii) Terms and conditions of employment[17]

The concept of "terms and conditions of employment" is further specified by the Recommendation (Paragraph 2(b)), which enumerates the following areas: advancement in accordance with individual character, experience, ability and diligence of the person concerned; security of tenure of employment; remuneration for work of equal value; and conditions of work "including hours of work, rest periods, annual holidays with pay, occupational safety and occupational health measures, as well as social security measures and welfare facilities and benefits provided in connection with employment". The concept of terms and conditions of employment is therefore broader than that of general conditions of work which it encompasses.

Promotion consists of the right of every individual not to be subject to any discrimination based on any of the grounds set out in the Convention as regards promotion earned in the course of employment.

Security of tenure denotes the guarantee that dismissal must not take place on discriminatory grounds, but must be justified by reasons connected with the worker's conduct, his or her ability or fitness to perform the functions or the strict necessities of the operation of the enterprise.

Equal remuneration. This principle, which is covered in relation to men and women by the Equal Remuneration Convention, 1951 (No. 100), supplemented by Recommendation No. 90, presupposes a general context which is free from inequality. The relation between the principle set forth in Convention No. 100 and that of Convention No. 111 is therefore paramount in this respect. Convention No. 111 extends this principle to other grounds upon which discrimination is prohibited.

Collective negotiations and industrial relations. The parties should respect the principle of equality of opportunity and treatment in employment and occupation, and should ensure that collective agreements contain no provisions of a discriminatory character in respect of access to, training for, advancement in or retention of employment or in respect of the terms and conditions of employment.

Social security. Bearing in mind Article 5 of the Convention, any distinction made on the basis of sex which is not justified by special measures of protection or assistance either provided for in other international labour Conventions, or generally recognized as necessary, should be eliminated. Any discriminatory treatment in respect of benefits or conditions of entitlement to social security, the application of compulsory or voluntary statutory or occupational schemes, contributions and the calculation of benefits should be eliminated.

Other conditions of employment. These may include measures for the protection of workers' privacy, occupational safety and health measures, and the working environment.

(c) Measures not deemed to be discrimination

There are three categories of measures that are not considered to be discrimination under the Convention:

(1) those based on inherent requirements of a particular job;

(2) those warranted by the protection of the security of the State; and

(3) measures of protection and assistance.

(i) Inherent requirements of the job[18]

Under Article 2 of the Convention, "any distinction, exclusion or preference in respect of a particular job based on the inherent requirements thereof shall not be deemed to be discrimination". This exception must be interpreted restrictively. The Convention requires that access to training, employment and occupation be based on objective criteria defined in the light of academic and occupational qualifications required for the activity in question. When qualifications are required for a particular job, it may not be simple to distinguish between what does and what does not constitute discrimination. It is often difficult to draw the line between bona fide requirements for a job and the use of certain criteria to exclude certain categories of workers.

It appears from the preparatory work for the Convention that the concept of "a particular job" refers to a specific and definable job, function or task. The necessary qualifications may be defined as those required by the characteristics of the particular job in proportion to its inherent requirements. A genuine qualification, even if based on one of the criteria in the Convention, may not come into conflict with the principle of equality of opportunity and treatment. In no circumstances, however, may the same qualification be required for an entire sector of activity. Systematic application of requirements involving one or more of the grounds of discrimination set out in the Convention is inadmissible. Careful examination of each individual case is required. Similarly, the exclusion of certain jobs or occupations based on one of the grounds listed is contrary to the Convention.

There are few instances where the grounds listed in the Convention may actually constitute inherent requirements of the job. As regards men and women, distinctions on the basis of sex may be required for certain jobs, such as those in the performing arts, or those involving particular physical intimacy. With respect to religion, restrictions for some jobs associated with a particular religious institution may be acceptable. Political opinion may in certain limited circumstances constitute a bona fide qualification for certain senior policy-making positions.

(ii) Measures affecting an individual suspected of activities prejudicial to the security of the State (Article 4 of the Convention)[19]

In order to avoid undue limitations on the protection which the Convention seeks to guarantee, the exception set out in Article 4 must be applied strictly.

In the first place, Article 4 covers measures taken in respect of activities of which an individual is justifiably suspected or convicted with the exclusion of mere membership of a particular group or community.

Secondly, it covers activities that may be qualified as prejudicial to the security of the State, whether such activities are proven or whether consistent and precise elements justify suspicion of such activities.

Thirdly, measures intended to safeguard the security of the State must be sufficiently well defined and delimited to ensure that they do not become discrimination based on political opinion or religion.

With respect to the requirement of a procedural safeguard of appeal, there should be a "body to which appeals can be made, which should therefore be independent from administrative or governmental authorities, and a mere right of appeal to the administrative or governmental authority hierarchically above the authority that took the measure is not enough; this body should offer guarantees of independence and impartiality; it must be 'competent' to assess fully the substance of the matter: that is, it should be in a position to ascertain the reasons underlying the measures taken, and give the appellant facilities for fully presenting his or her case".[20]

(iii) Special measures of protection or assistance (Article 5 of the Convention)[21]

Measures provided for in international labour standards. The ratification of Convention No. 111 must not come into conflict with the ratification or implementation of other instruments adopted by the ILO that provide for special measures of protection or assistance. This is the case, for example, of special measures taken on behalf of indigenous peoples, persons with disabilities or older persons, as well as measures to protect maternity or the health of women.

Measures designed to meet the particular requirements of certain categories of persons. These are measures that may be determined by any member State, after consultation with representative employers' and workers' organizations, and which are generally recognized to be necessary for reasons such as age, disablement, family responsibilities or social or cultural status. This provision is designed, on the one hand, to avoid conflicts between these special measures and the general policy to eliminate discrimination and, on the other hand, to allow special measures to secure equality of opportunity and treatment in practice, taking into account the diversity of situations of certain categories of persons.

(d) Implementation of the principles:
The obligations of States[22]

The implementation of the principles of the Convention consists primarily of declaring and pursuing a national policy designed to promote equality of opportunity and treatment in respect of employment and occupation, both directly, by ensuring its observance in services and employment under the control of a national authority, and indirectly, by taking measures to secure its acceptance in other sectors.

(i) Formulation and content of the national policy designed to promote equality of opportunity and treatment (Article 2 of the Convention)[23]

Article 2 provides that this national policy must promote equality "by methods appropriate to national conditions and practice", thereby allowing States considerable flexibility in the manner in which it is declared and pursued, which is not subject to any predetermined form.

The policy must, however, be clearly stated, which implies that programmes for this purpose should be developed and implemented, and appropriate measures adopted according to the principles outlined in Article 3 of the Convention and Paragraph 2 of the Recommendation. While the mere affirmation of the principle of equality before the law may be an element of such a policy, it cannot in itself constitute a policy within the meaning of Article 2 of the Convention.

There are also certain immediate obligations, such as repealing discriminatory legal provisions and putting an end to discriminatory administrative practices, as well as the obligation to supply reports on the results achieved.

The realization of the policy is recognized to be progress and in all likelihood requires continuous implementation and monitoring.

(ii) Obligations for the implementation of a national policy of equality of opportunity and treatment (Article 3 of the Convention)[24]

Article 3 of the Convention specifies some of the areas and means of action which must be covered by the national policy to promote equality in employment and occupation. It sets out obligations of various types, either immediate, or to which effect may be given more progressively.

The immediate obligations include:

- repealing any statutory provisions and modifying any administrative instructions or practices which are inconsistent with the policy of equality (Article 3(c));

- pursuing the policy in respect of employment under the direct control of a national authority (Article 3(d)); and

Equality of opportunity and treatment

- ensuring observance of the policy in the activities of vocational guidance, vocational training and placement services under the direction of a national authority (Article 3(e)).

The medium-term obligations are as follows:

- to enact legislation and promote educational programmes as may be calculated to secure the acceptance and observance of the policy (Article 3(b)); and
- to cooperate with employers' and workers' organizations in promoting the acceptance and observance of the policy (Article 3(a)).

(iii) National machinery to promote application of the policy

Paragraph 4 of the Recommendation provides for the establishment of agencies, to be assisted where practicable by advisory committees composed of representatives of employers' and workers' organizations, and of other interested bodies, for the purpose of promoting application of the policy in all fields of public and private employment, and in particular:

(a) to take all practicable measures to foster public understanding and acceptance of the principles of non-discrimination;

(b) to receive, examine and investigate complaints that the policy is not being observed and, if necessary by conciliation, to secure the correction of any practices regarded as in conflict with the policy; and

(c) to consider further any complaints which cannot be effectively settled by conciliation and to render opinions or issue decisions concerning the manner in which discriminatory practices revealed should be corrected.

5.2.2 Equal remuneration: The Equal Remuneration Convention (No. 100), and Recommendation (No. 90), 1951

(a) Persons covered and definitions

(i) Workers

The Convention covers "all workers" and "men and women workers" without limitation. The Convention therefore applies in general to all sectors, both public and private (Article 2).

(ii) Remuneration[25]

According to Article 1(a) of the Convention "the term 'remuneration' includes the ordinary, basic or minimum wage or salary and any additional emoluments whatsoever payable directly or indirectly, whether in cash or in kind, by the employer to the worker and arising out of the worker's employment". This definition is couched in the broadest possible terms with a view to ensuring that equality is not limited to the basic or ordinary wage, nor in any other way restricted according to semantic distinctions. It is important to emphasize that the principle set forth in the Convention covers both the minimum wage and remuneration determined in any other way.

Additional emoluments. The term "any additional emoluments whatsoever" is also all-embracing and includes increments based on seniority or marital status, cost-of-living allowances, housing or residential allowances, family allowances and benefits in kind, such as the provision and laundering of working clothes provided by the employer.

Indirect elements of remuneration. The term "directly or indirectly" covers certain indirect elements of remuneration which are not payable directly by the employer, but which arise out of the employment relationship. They may include allowances paid out of a common fund managed by employers or workers.

Arising out of the worker's employment. A link between the worker's employment and the payments must be established. Allowances paid under social security systems financed by the undertaking or industries concerned are considered an element of remuneration. Allowances paid under a social security system financed entirely by public funds are not considered to be remuneration and thus are outside the scope of the Convention.

(iii) Work of equal value[26]

Article 1(b) of the Convention provides that the expression refers to rates of remuneration established without discrimination based on sex. By situating the comparison at the level of the "value" of work, Convention No. 100 and Recommendation No. 90 go beyond a reference to "the same" or "similar" work and cover different jobs to which the same value may be attributed. Value, while not defined specifically in the Convention, refers to the worth of the job for purposes of computing remuneration. The Convention does not limit application of the concept of equal value to implementation through the methodology of comparable worth, but it certainly indicates that something other than market forces should be used to ensure application of the principle. It suggests that objective job appraisals should be used to determine valuation where deemed useful, on the basis of the work to be performed and not on the basis of the sex of the jobholder. While job appraisal systems are still a common feature of wage setting, other bases for the calculation of wages – including minimum wages, productivity pay and new competency-based wage systems – are covered by the Convention.

(b) The role of governments in the application of the principle of equal remuneration[27]

The obligation of a State which has ratified the Convention is a function of the wage-determination machinery in force in the country. The State's obligation to *ensure* the implementation of the principle of equal remuneration is limited to those areas where such action is consistent with the methods in operation for determining rates of remuneration, in other words where the State is directly or indirectly involved in wage fixing. In areas where the government does not intervene either directly or indirectly in the negotiation of wages, its obligation is to *promote* the application of the principle.

(c) Means of giving effect to the Convention

Article 2, paragraph 2, of the Convention provides that the principle of equal remuneration for men and women workers for work of equal value may be applied by means of:

(a) *national laws or regulations.* While there is no general obligation to enact legislation under the Convention, any existing legislative provision which violates the principle of equal remuneration must be amended or repealed; or

(b) *any legally established or recognized machinery for wage determination.* In many countries there are bodies at the national level responsible for determining the applicable wage levels, and they should do so in accordance with the Convention. The composition of these bodies and the criteria used are often determining factors in the application of the principle. The minimum wage is also an important means of applying the principle of equal remuneration; or

(c) *collective agreements concluded between employers and workers.* Remuneration rates are often covered by collective agreements concluded between employers and workers, and should be established in conformity with the Convention. These can make an effective contribution to the application of the principle; or

(d) *a combination of these various means.*

(d) Objective evaluation of jobs[28]

Article 3, paragraph 1, of the Convention calls for measures to be taken to promote objective appraisal of jobs on the basis of the work to be performed "where such action will assist in giving effect to the provisions of this Convention". Job evaluation provides a way of systematically classifying jobs according to their content and the skills required, without regard to the sex or personal characteristics of the worker.

(e) The role of employers' and workers' organizations[29]

Under the terms of Article 4 of the Convention, "each Member shall cooperate as appropriate with the employers' and workers' organisations concerned for the purpose of giving effect to the provisions of this Convention". Paragraph 5 of Recommendation No. 90 provides that employers' and workers' organizations should participate in the establishment of methods of job evaluation where appropriate. These provisions also indicate the share in the responsibility incumbent upon employers' and workers' organizations for the effective application of the principle of equal remuneration.

5.3 SUMMARY OF THE PRINCIPLES OF THE COMMITTEE OF EXPERTS

Certain principles relating to the application of the Conventions, which are not explicitly set out in the instruments, have also been developed in the comments of the Committee of Experts.

5.3.1 Discrimination in employment and occupation: Convention No. 111 and Recommendation No. 111

(a) Grounds of discrimination

The Convention covers any direct or indirect discrimination, whether it is in law, resulting from the legislation, or in practice, including the practice of private individuals.

(i) *Race and colour.* In the protection against discrimination based on race and colour, the main problem is not so much to define the terms employed, as to eradicate the negative values that the perpetrators of discrimination attribute to the person discriminated against. In such cases, and especially through the use of positive measures, state policies should be aimed at making equality of opportunity a reality for every population group.[30]

(ii) *National extraction.* The Committee of Experts has stressed that the elimination of discrimination on grounds of national extraction along with other grounds is critical to sustainable development, all the more so because of the re-emergence of signs of intolerance and racism. Steps should be taken to raise public awareness and promote tolerance, respect and understanding between ethnic communities and throughout society. These grounds include national ethnic and linguistic minority groups.[31]

(iii) *Religion.* The Convention aims to provide protection against discrimination in employment and occupation on the basis of religion, which is often the consequence of a lack of freedom or intolerance. Situations that may lead to religious discrimination derive more from an attitude of intolerance towards persons who profess a particular religion, or no religion, and may be linked to multi-ethnic communities. The risk of discrimination often arises from the absence of religious belief or from belief in different ethical principles, from lack of religious freedom, in particular where one religion has been established as the religion of the State, where the State is officially anti-religious, or where the dominant political doctrine is hostile to all religions. In a great majority of cases, discrimination on grounds of religion is not institutionalized. The freedom to practise a religion can be hindered by the constraints of a trade or occupation, particularly in regard to the manifestation of discrimi-

Equality of opportunity and treatment

nation, including practices, affiliation, membership, clothing and attendance at ceremonies. This may happen when a religion prohibits work on a different day of rest established by law or custom, or where there are requirements of particular clothing. In these cases, the workers' right to practise his or her faith or belief needs to be weighed against the need to meet the requirements inherent in the job or the operational requirements. The rights may be restricted within the limits imposed by the principle of proportionality.[32]

(iv) *Social origin.* Prejudices and preferences based on social origin may persist when a rigid division of society into classes determines an individual's opportunities in employment and occupation, or when certain "castes" are considered to be inferior and are therefore confined to the most menial jobs.

(v) *Sex.* The criterion of sex covers distinctions based on biological characteristics and functions that differentiate men and women, as well as distinctions based on social differences between men and women that are learned, changeable over time and have wide variations within and between cultures. Use of the concept of gender as a socio-economic variable to analyse roles, responsibilities, constraints, opportunities and needs of men and women is essential to promote equal opportunity and treatment under the Convention.

The Committee of Experts has noted that discrimination against women may take many forms which at first appear to be sex neutral but which actually constitute discrimination because they have a detrimental impact on women. For example, in matters of access to and retention of employment, criteria related to marital status, family situation and family responsibilities typically affect only women to their detriment in employment.

(vi) *Political opinion.* The Committee of Experts has indicated that, in protecting workers against discrimination with regard to employment and occupation on the basis of political opinion, the Convention implies that this protection shall be afforded to them in respect of activities expressing or demonstrating opposition to the established political principles – since the protection of opinions which are neither expressed nor demonstrated would be pointless. Regarding the nature of the opinions expressed, the Committee has noted that "the protection afforded by the Convention is not limited to differences of opinion within the framework of established principles. Therefore, even if certain doctrines are aimed at fundamental changes in the institutions of the State, this does not constitute a reason for considering their propagation beyond the protection of the Convention, in the absence of the use or advocacy of violent methods to bring about that result". The Committee of Experts recalls the opinion expressed by a Commission of Inquiry appointed under article 26 of the Constitution of the ILO that:

> ... the protection of freedom of expression is aimed not merely at the individual's intellectual satisfaction at being able to speak his [or her] mind, but rather – and especially as regards the expression of political opinions – at giving him [or her] an opportunity to seek to influence decisions in the political, economic and social life of his [or her] society. For his [or her] political views to have an impact, the individual generally acts in conjunction with others. Political organizations and parties constitute a framework within which the members seek to secure wider acceptance of their opinions. To be meaningful, the protection of political opinions must therefore extend to their collective advocacy within such entities. Measures taken against a person by reference to the aims of an organization or party to which he [or she] belongs imply that he [or she] must not associate himself [or herself] with those aims, and accordingly restrict his [or her] freedom to manifest his [or her] opinions.

The Committee of Experts has also noted that:

> ... one of the essential traits of this type of discrimination is that it is most likely to be due to measures taken by the State or the public authorities. Its effects may be felt in the public services, but are not confined thereto; moreover, in many modern economies the distinction between the public and private sector has become blurred or has disappeared completely.[33]

(vii) *Additional grounds.* In its Special Survey of 1996,[34] the Committee of Experts recommended that consideration be given to the adoption of an additional Protocol to the annex to the Convention, the objective of which would be to include additional criteria on the basis of which discrimination would be prohibited. The Committee of Experts considered that the following criteria are broadly accepted and merit consideration for inclusion in the additional Protocol (listed in alphabetical order): age, disability, family responsibilities, language, matrimonial status, nationality, property, sexual orientation, state of health,[35] and trade union affiliation.

(b) The elimination of discrimination, legislation and practical application[36]

There are several regulatory levels at which the Convention can be implemented nationally: the national constitution, legislation, case law and collective labour agreements. Where provisions are adopted to give effect to the Convention, they should include all seven grounds of discrimination specified in article 1, paragraph 1(a).

The Committee has reiterated that legislation is essential, but in itself is not sufficient to apply the Convention. No society is free from discrimination and a denial of its existence is a serious obstacle to addressing it and to making progress in promoting equality of opportunity and treatment. The application of the principles of the Convention is achieved in successive stages, each stage being the occasion for perspectives revealing new and different problems, thereby resulting in the taking of new measures to resolve them.[37]

Equality of opportunity and treatment

(c) **The obligation of the State to apply a national policy to promote equality in employment under the direct control of a national authority**[38]

With respect to the establishment and promotion of a national policy, the Committee of Experts has recalled that, while the inclusion in a Constitution of the principle of equality of opportunity and treatment and the judicial protection of victims of discrimination represents an important stage in the implementation of the above principle, they cannot on their own constitute a national policy within the meaning of Article 2 of the Convention. The implementation of a policy of equality of opportunity and treatment also presupposes the adoption of specific measures designed to correct inequalities observed in practice. Indeed, the promotion of equality of opportunity and treatment in employment and occupation as advocated by the Convention is not aimed at a stable situation which can be definitively attained, but at a permanent process in the course of which the national equality policy must continually be adjusted to the changes that it brings about in society. While the Convention leaves it to each country to intervene according to the methods which appear to be the most adequate, taking into account national circumstances and customs, the effective application of the national policy of equality of opportunity and treatment requires the implementation by the State concerned of appropriate measures, the underlying principles of which are enumerated in Article 3 of the Convention. It is therefore important to emphasize the interdependence of these two means of action, consisting of the adoption of legal provisions, and the preparation and implementation of programmes to promote equality and correct de facto inequalities which may exist in training, employment and conditions of work.[39]

The Committee stresses that the Convention, in addition to legislative measures, requires the government to pursue national policy through positive measures with a view to eliminating discrimination on all grounds contained in the Convention. The collection of statistical data is part of an effective policy to promote equality as it allows for targeted action to be taken.[40]

The use of the methods of direct application of the policy available to the States is one of the obligations laid down by the Convention. Governments are encouraged to adopt programmes of affirmative action, thereby responding to the concern to increase the overall number of members of disadvantaged groups in the service, as a means of ensuring their participation at all levels of the service, including the higher levels. Affirmative action programmes focus not only on recruitment policy, but also on issues related to training in employment which, to a great extent, determine promotion policy. The execution of public contracts is also an area in which the public authorities may have means of directly influencing employment practices. The Committee of Experts recommends examining the possibility of including clauses providing for equality of opportunity and treatment in public contracts. It also encourages governments to make all possible efforts to allocate adequate resources to institutions and structures responsible for promoting equality.

(d) Cooperation with employers' and workers' organizations[41]

The requirement in this respect is for active collaboration with the above organizations. It is generally sought for the preparation and supervision of the application of the measures adopted within the context of the national policy envisaged in Article 2 of the Convention, as well as subsequently at the sectoral, enterprise or establishment level for the direct application of the principles set out in the Convention. This collaboration goes beyond mere consultation with employers' and workers' organizations, and must therefore allow real consideration of the positions of the various parties.

(e) Special measures of protection or assistance

Article 5 of the Convention envisages two kinds of special measures of protection and assistance: measures of protection and assistance provided for in international labour Conventions and Recommendations; and measures taken after consultation with employers' and workers' organizations and designed to meet the particular requirements of persons who require special protection or assistance.

(i) Measures provided for in international labour standards[42]

Article 5, paragraph 1, of the Convention provides that the "special measures of protection or assistance provided for in other Conventions or Recommendations adopted by the International Labour Conference shall not be deemed to be discrimination". This concerns, for instance, special measures which may be taken on behalf of indigenous or tribal peoples, or workers with disabilities or older persons, as well as those designed to protect maternity or the health of women, and which are expressly recognized as non-discriminatory. Thus, the Conference's standard-setting activity cannot be considered as establishing or permitting discrimination within the meaning of the 1958 instruments. Consequently, the ratification and application of Convention No. 111 should not come into conflict with the ratification or implementation of other instruments providing for special measures of protection or assistance.

For example, maternity is a condition which requires differential treatment to achieve genuine equality and, in this sense, it is more of a premise of the principle of equality than a dispensation. Special maternity protection measures should be taken to enable women to fulfil their maternal role without being marginalized in the labour market.

Under Convention No. 111, the Committee of Experts has reiterated that maternity protection measures are not in violation of the Convention

Equality of opportunity and treatment

and that other "protective" measures should be reviewed in accordance with the Resolution on equal opportunities and equal treatment for men and women in employment, adopted by the International Labour Conference in 1985, which recommended that all protective legislation applying to women should be reviewed in the light of up-to-date scientific knowledge and technical changes and that it should be revised, supplemented, extended, retained or repealed, according to national circumstances. As for ILO standards, it requested that protective instruments, such as Convention No. 89, be reviewed periodically to determine whether their provisions were still adequate and appropriate in the light of experience acquired since their adoption, and of scientific and technical information and social progress.

The Committee considers that recognition of the principle of equality between men and women is intended not only to eliminate legal provisions and practices which create advantages and disadvantages on the basis of sex, but also to achieve now and in the future effective equality of rights for both sexes by equalizing their conditions of employment and their roles in society so that women can enjoy the same employment opportunities as men. For this reason, differences in treatment between men and women can only be permitted on an exceptional basis, that is, when they promote effective equality in society between the sexes, thereby correcting previous discriminatory practices, or where they are justified by the existence, and therefore the persistence, of overriding biological or physiological reasons, as in the case of pregnancy and maternity in particular. This requires a critical re-examination of provisions that are assumed to be "protective" towards women, but that in fact have the effect of hindering the achievement of effective equality by perpetuating or consolidating their disadvantaged employment situation.

(ii) Measures designed to meet the particular requirements of certain persons

The Convention permits the adoption of special measures designed to meet the particular requirements of persons who, for reasons such as sex, age, disablement, family responsibilities or social or cultural status, are generally recognized to require special protection or assistance.

In applying the 1958 instruments, it is important to ensure that the special measures concerned do in fact pursue the objective of offering protection or assistance. These special measures tend to ensure equality of opportunity and treatment in practice, taking into account the diversity of situations of certain persons, so as to halt discriminatory practices against them and promote equality. These types of preferential treatment are thus designed to restore a balance and are or should be part of a broader effort to eliminate all inequalities.

Because of the aim of protection and assistance which they are to pursue, these special measures must be proportional to the nature and scope of the protection needed or of the existing discrimination. A careful re-examination of certain measures may reveal that they are conducive to establishing or permitting actual distinctions, exclusions or preferences falling under Article 1 of the Convention. For this reason, consultation with employers' and workers' organizations, where they exist, constitutes a significant guarantee when such measures are being formulated. Such consultation must ensure that a careful examination of the measures concerned has been undertaken before they are defined as non-discriminatory and that the representative employers' and workers' organizations have had an opportunity to express their opinions on the matter. Once adopted, the special measures should be re-examined periodically, in order to ascertain whether they are still needed and remain effective. It should be borne in mind that such measures are clearly of a temporary nature inasmuch as their objective is to compensate for imbalances resulting from discrimination against certain workers or certain sectors. Such measures may take the form of positive or affirmative action for disadvantaged groups.

The following grounds may call for the adoption of special measures of protection or assistance: sex, age, disablement, or membership of an ethnic minority, or of indigenous and tribal peoples; this list is not exhaustive and must be adapted to national circumstances.

5.3.2 Equal remuneration: Convention No. 100 and Recommendation No. 90

(a) Means of giving effect to the Convention[43]

The marked progress in the application of the principle that has been noted by the Committee of Experts includes the recognition by countries of the very broad definition of remuneration contained in Convention No. 100, which seeks to ensure that equality is not limited to the basic or ordinary wage. Increasingly, countries are extending protections of equality in law and practice to ensure that additional payments and fringe benefits such as uniforms, housing, travel allowances and dependency allowances are included in the definition of remuneration and are not differentiated on the basis of sex. In those countries where pay levels are linked closely to seniority, the Committee has suggested that consideration might be given to allowing women a seniority credit for time taken out of the workforce to care for family members. At the very least, seniority levels should not be lost for taking maternity or family leave. Some new laws, in addition to setting out the principle of the Convention, also provide that the various components of remuneration must be established according to identical standards for men and for women, that professional categories and classifications and the criteria for promotion must be common to workers of both sexes, and that methods for the evaluation of jobs must be based on objective and identical criteria, and essentially on the nature of the work involved. The Committee has noted positive action measures taken by a number of ratifying

States to implement the Convention in practice. Some examples of these include the adoption of codes of conduct, equal pay plans, pay equity councils, pay valuation guides, modernization of public personnel classification schemes, undertaking of job evaluation exercises, undertaking of surveys to identify areas of wage differentials, and granting of pay equity benefits to compensate for past pay differentials based on sex. Many countries have established and extended minimum wages and/or issued guidelines on wage levels generally. Although not expressly required under Convention No. 100, the setting of minimum wages is an important means by which the Convention is applied.

(b) Methods of job evaluation[44]

The adoption of the concept of equal remuneration for work of equal value necessarily implies some comparison between jobs. The Committee has stated, in this regard, that the scope of comparison should be as wide as is allowed for by the wage system in existence. As men and women tend to perform different jobs, in order to eliminate wage discrimination on the basis of sex, it is essential to establish appropriate techniques and procedures to measure the relative value of jobs with varying content. The Convention does not favour any particular method of evaluation. However, many countries use the analytical job evaluation methodology and there is a growing consensus that it is the most practicable method of ensuring the application of the principle of equal remuneration in practice. What the Committee is most concerned about and does advocate, is that the utmost care be taken in including factors to take sufficiently into account jobs commonly regarded as being carried out by women, so that the degree of subjectivity and gender bias is minimized.

The Committee has therefore stressed that care should be taken to prevent sex stereotyping from entering the job evaluation process, as this may result in an under-evaluation of tasks performed primarily by women or those perceived as intrinsically "feminine". It is therefore essential to take measures to ensure that job evaluations are carried out on the basis of objective criteria. These criteria should not undervalue skills normally required for jobs that are in practice performed by women, such as providing care, manual dexterity and human relations skills, nor should they overvalue those attributes, such as physical strength, typically associated with jobs traditionally performed by men. The qualities most often attributed to women tend to be undervalued by society in comparison with those qualities that men are said to possess. Not surprisingly, societal values are also reflected in wage systems. Many traditional job evaluation systems also show an obvious gender bias by undervaluing or ignoring the support and non-managerial work often performed by women.

(c) The implementation of job evaluation

The participation of all the social partners is essential for the implementation of the comparison of jobs. The involvement of occupational organizations must therefore be secured with the common objective of achieving wage equality in full knowledge of the situation, that is following appropriate training on the concept of wage discrimination and in awareness that it has to be eliminated.

(d) Statistics[45]

In a general observation in 1999, the Committee of Experts noted that more complete information is required in order to permit an adequate evaluation of the nature, extent and causes of the pay differential between men and women, and the progress achieved in implementing the principle of the Convention. Accordingly, in order to assist the Committee in evaluating the application of the principle of equal remuneration, and in accordance with the provisions of the Labour Statistics Convention, 1985 (No. 160), the Committee asks the governments to provide the fullest possible statistical information, disaggregated by sex, in their reports, with regard to the following:

- the distribution of men and women in the public sector, the federal and/or state civil service, and in the private sector by earning levels and hours of work (defined as hours actually worked or hours paid for), classified by: (1) branch of economic activity; (2) occupation or occupational group or level of education/qualification; (3) seniority; (4) age group; (5) number of hours actually worked or paid for, and where relevant, by (6) size of enterprise and (7) geographical area; and

- statistical data on the composition of earnings (indicating the nature of earnings, such as basic, ordinary or minimum wage or salary, premium pay for overtime and shift differentials, allowances, bonuses and gratuities, and remuneration for time not worked) and hours of work (defined as hours actually worked or paid for), classified according to the same variables as the distribution of employees (subparagraphs (1) to (7) above).

Where feasible, statistics on average earnings should be compiled according to hours actually worked or paid for, with an indication of the concept of hours of work used. Where earnings data are compiled on a different basis (e.g. earnings per week or per month), the statistics on the average number of hours of work should refer to the same time period (that is, by week or by month).

With respect to the fact that some governments are not yet in a position to provide full statistical information, the Committee of Experts asked them to supply all the information that is currently available to them and to continue to work towards the compilation of the statistical information set out above.

Equality of opportunity and treatment

(e) A comprehensive approach[46]

The Committee of Experts has long taken the view that wage discrimination cannot be tackled effectively unless action is also taken simultaneously to deal with all of its sources. As is evident from the preceding discussion, it is important to discuss equal remuneration and job evaluation in the context of a more general protection against discrimination, such as that offered in the Discrimination (Employment and Occupation) Convention, 1958 (No. 111), and the Workers with Family Responsibilities Convention, 1981 (No. 156). The Committee continues to emphasize that a comprehensive approach to the reduction and elimination of pay disparities between men and women, involving societal, political, cultural and labour market interventions, is required. The Committee believes that the application of the principle of equal pay for work of equal value should be an explicit and necessary part of such a strategy as it has advantages that non-labour market strategies appear unable to achieve on their own. The Committee has noted that the adoption of adequate legislation requiring equal pay for work of equal value is important, but is insufficient to achieve the goals of the Convention. Policies that deal only with labour market discrimination are inadequate, since factors arising outside the labour market (relating to traditional ideas about the role of women and the conflict between work and family responsibilities) appear to be a more significant source of pay inequality than factors that originate within the labour market. The continued persistence of the wage gap requires that governments, along with social partners, take more proactive measures to raise awareness, make assessments, and promote and enforce application of the principle of equal pay for work of equal value.

5.4 PRACTICAL DIFFICULTIES AND PRINCIPAL OBSTACLES IN THE APPLICATION OF THE CONVENTIONS

5.4.1 Discrimination in employment and occupation: Convention No. 111 and Recommendation No. 111

In many States which have adopted appropriate legislation in respect of promoting equality of opportunity and treatment in employment and eliminating discrimination, the Committee of Experts has noted that the practical implementation of the legislation and the national policy still give rise to many and varied difficulties. Even in States in which the Constitution and other legal provisions explicitly prohibit discrimination, particularly on the basis of sex, in practice concrete and affirmative measures are required, without which the achievement of equality is impossible. Cultural and economic factors are also at the basis of discriminatory practices based on race and religion, which are still very common in relation to access to employment and which occur in States where strict regulations have been adopted in this respect, combined with penal sanctions.

(a) Covering of all the criteria set out in the Convention, and of all workers

The Committee of Experts has noted that in certain countries the legislation does not prohibit discrimination in employment based on all the criteria set forth in the Convention, or that the protection does not extend to all workers. The Committee has indicated that it is essential, when reviewing the position and deciding on the measures to be taken, that governments should give their attention to all the grounds of discrimination envisaged in the 1958 instruments.[47] In cases where certain categories of workers (such as public servants, certain agricultural workers, domestic workers) are excluded from the scope of the general legislation applicable to workers, and particularly the protection afforded by the Labour Code, it is important to ensure that the protection afforded to these workers under the terms of the Convention is secured through provisions that are applicable to them.

(b) Implementation of a national policy to promote equality of opportunity and treatment

The Committee of Experts has noted that a number of governments indicate that the Convention does not give rise to difficulties or is fully applied, without providing other information on the content or means by which the national policy is applied. Such a statement is difficult to accept,[48] since the quality of opportunity and treatment cannot be achieved in a stable and definitive manner, but requires a permanent and progressive process during which the national policy has to adjust to changes in society and evolve on the basis of the progress achieved in the implementation of the principle in law and practice. Indeed, there remains a broad range of discrimination in most States, based not only on sex but also, and in particular, on race, religion and political opinion.

Other difficulties in the full application of the Convention include the fear of reprisals, the burden of proof, ineffective sanctions and remedies, the non-availability of legal assistance and inadequate institutions to safeguard equality rights.

5.4.2. Equal remuneration: Convention No. 100 and Recommendation No. 90

(a) Individual scope of the instruments

As provided for in Article 2, paragraph 1, of Convention No. 100, the principle set out in the Convention applies to all workers. Nevertheless, as in the case of application of Convention No. 111, significant categories of workers, and generally those earning wages near to or lower than the minimum wage, are often excluded from the legal protection afforded against wage discrimination. The question therefore arises as to the protection of these categories of workers who are excluded from legal protection.

Equality of opportunity and treatment

(b) Meaning of the concept of "work of equal value"

Although the concept of work of "equal value", which goes beyond references to identical work performed by persons with the same skills, the same experience and working under the same conditions, has been adopted in a significant number of countries, its interpretation, and therefore its application, give rise to many difficulties. The narrow concept of equal pay for equal work has been outdated since the end of the Second World War, in spite of the fact that it found its way into the Universal Declaration of Human Rights. If the equal pay principle were defined in such a way, its application would be extremely limited, since few people perform the same work and men and women perform, to a considerable extent, very different jobs. In fact, the drafters of the Convention, while noting the difficulty associated with the application of equal value, never shied away from insisting on its use as the guiding principle.

(c) Job evaluation

The Committee of Experts has recognized that several difficulties exist, which hinder the use of job evaluation in the promotion of the Convention. In some countries, wages are fixed in an ad hoc manner or through bargaining without the use of any job evaluation methodology. Secondly, carrying out job evaluation exercises, as well as undertaking studies and taking steps to equalize wages, costs time and money. Finally, everywhere job evaluation exercises are carried out, they may not incorporate necessary measures to reduce gender bias in the evaluation so as to ensure an objective appraisal of jobs in accordance with the Convention.

(d) Statistics[49]

Statistical information is of great importance in the evaluation of inequalities which exist in the labour market between men and women, and the development of strategies to address these inequalities. It is therefore necessary to have available the most complete statistics possible, on the one hand, to make it possible to undertake an adequate evaluation of the nature, extent and cause of wage differentials between men and women, and on the other hand, to be able to evaluate the progress achieved in the application of the Convention. Moreover, the Committee of Experts has emphasized that an analysis of the position and pay of men and women in all job categories and between the various sectors is required to address fully the continuing remuneration gap between men and women which is based on sex. The Committee of Experts, noting the lack of adequate data, has recommended the manner in which statistics would have to be collected in order to undertake such an assessment. Governments have therefore been urged to analyse the national situation in order to determine the extent and the nature of the pay gap, by sector if possible, as a starting point in addressing the equal pay issue.

Fundamental rights at work and international labour standards

Table 5.1 Instruments on non-discrimination and equality of opportunity and treatment in employment and occupation

Instruments	Number of ratifications (31 August 2002)	Status
Up-to-date instruments (Conventions whose ratification is encouraged and Recommendations to which member States are invited to give effect.)		
Equal Remuneration Convention, 1951 (No. 100)	159	**Fundamental Convention.**
Equal Remuneration Recommendation, 1951 (No. 90)	–	This Recommendation is related to a fundamental Convention and is considered up to date.
Discrimination (Employment and Occupation) Convention, 1958 (No. 111)	156	**Fundamental Convention.**
Discrimination (Employment and Occupation) Recommendation, 1958 (No. 111)	–	This Recommendation is related to a fundamental Convention and is considered up to date.
Outdated instruments (Instruments that are no longer up to date; this category includes the Conventions that member States are no longer invited to ratify and the Recommendations whose implementation is no longer encouraged.)		
In the area of equality in employment and occupation and equal remuneration, no instrument has been considered as outdated by the Governing Body.		

(e) The causes of wage differentials[50]

It is now recognized that the causes of pay differentials between men and women are found both within and outside the labour market. Many difficulties encountered in achieving equal remuneration are closely linked to the general status of women and men in employment and society. The male/female wage gap has been traced mainly to the following factors: lower, less appropriate and less career-oriented education, training and skills levels; horizontal and vertical occupational segregation of women into lower-paying jobs or occupations and lower-level positions without promotion opportunities; household and family responsibilities; perceived costs of employing women; and pay structures. In some countries, particularly in the agricultural sector, collective agreements may still reflect male and female pay rates and, in some countries, differential productivity rates are set for men and women. The establishment of centralized minimum standards, narrow pay dispersion and transparency of pay structures have been identified as factors that could address the pay structure differences and help reduce the gender pay gap.

Equality of opportunity and treatment

Notes

[1] Preamble to the ILO Constitution. Emphasis was also placed on the protection of women, young persons and children.

[2] ILO: *Record of Proceedings*, International Labour Conference (ILC), 24th Session, Geneva, 1938, p. 679.

[3] Part II of the Declaration of Philadelphia which, according to article 1, para. 1, of the Constitution, sets forth the objectives of the ILO.

[4] ILC, 60th Session, 1975, Declaration on Equality of Opportunity and Treatment for Women Workers; ILO: *Official Bulletin*, Vol. LVIII, 1975, Series A, No. 1, pp. 96-100. The Declaration emphasizes that "all forms of discrimination on grounds of sex which deny or restrict [equality of opportunity and treatment for all workers] are unacceptable and must be eliminated". Convinced that the persistence of discrimination against women workers is incompatible with the interests of the economy and social justice, it states that the protection of women at work shall be an integral part of the efforts aimed at improving the living and working conditions of all employees, and that women shall be protected from risks inherent in their employment and occupation on the same basis and with the same standards of protection as men. It also emphasizes that positive special treatment during a transitional period aimed at effective equality between the sexes shall not be regarded as discriminatory.

[5] ILC, 71st Session, 1985, resolution and conclusions on equal opportunities and equal treatment for men and women in employment; ILO: *Official Bulletin*, Vol. LXVIII, 1985, Series A, No. 2, pp. 85-95: the conclusions review the policy and measures adopted by the ILO for women workers over the previous ten years, emphasizing the need to intensify the measures taken with a view to ensuring better conditions of employment, work and life for women, and to achieve their participation in all the aspects of the development process. The conclusions outline a series of measures to guide national action and that of the ILO in various fields and emphasize the specific problems encountered by rural women workers, the difficulties of reintegration into working life after a period of absence, and the difficulties of women belonging to underprivileged categories, such as migrant workers, refugees, the disabled, minorities, single-parent families and the long-term unemployed. The resolution concerning ILO action for women workers, adopted by the ILC in 1991, reaffirms the ILO's constant concern for women workers and recalls its resolution of 1985. It emphasizes that a concerted effort by governments and organizations of employers and workers remains necessary to give effect to the principle of equality. It therefore calls upon governments, as well as employers' and workers' organizations, to adopt comprehensive strategies to eliminate the continuing barriers to the equal participation of women in employment through the ratification of the relevant Conventions, and the adoption of policies and positive and concrete measures with a view to increasing the participation of women in all fields of employment, including decision-making.

[6] ILO: *Night work of women in industry*, General Survey by the Committee of Experts on the Application of Conventions and Recommendations, Report III (Part IB), ILC, 89th Session, 2001.

[7] ILO: *Equality in employment and occupation*, Special Survey on equality in employment and occupation in respect of Convention No. 111, Report III (Part 4B), ILC, 83rd Session, 1996, paras. 18-64.

[8] Under the terms of paragraph 8 of Recommendation No. 111, with respect to immigrant workers, regard should be had to the provisions of the Migration for Employment Convention (Revised), 1949 (No. 97), which was later supplemented by the Migrant Workers (Supplementary Provisions) Convention, 1975 (No. 143).

[9] ILO: *Equality in employment and occupation*, General Survey of the Reports on the Discrimination (Employment and Occupation) Convention (No. 111) and Recommendation (No. 111), 1958, Report III (Part 4B), ILC, 75th Session, 1988, paras. 22-29; ILO: *Equality ...*, Special Survey ..., 1996, op. cit., paras. 23-26.

[10] ILO: *Equality* ..., General Survey ..., 1988, op. cit., paras. 30-74.

[11] ibid., para. 36; and ILO: *Equality* ..., Special Survey ..., 1996, op. cit., paras. 33-34.

[12] ibid., paras. 35-40.

[13] ILO: *Equality* ..., General Survey ..., 1988, op. cit., para. 54; idem: *Equality* ..., Special Survey ..., 1996, op. cit., para. 43.

[14] ILO: *Equality* ..., General Survey ..., 1988, op. cit., paras. 76-123.

[15] ibid., paras. 77-85.

[16] ibid., paras. 86-106.

[17] ibid., paras. 107-123.

[18] ibid., paras. 125-133; ILO: *Equality* ..., Special Survey ..., 1996, op. cit., paras. 118-122.

[19] ILO: *Equality* ..., General Survey ..., 1988, op. cit., paras. 134-138.

[20] ILO: *Discrimination in respect of employment and occupation: Summary of Reports on Unratified Conventions and on Recommendations*, Report III (Part II), ILC, 47th Session, 1963, para. 48.

[21] ILO: *Equality* ..., General Survey ..., 1988, op. cit., paras. 139-155.

[22] ibid., paras. 157-236.

[23] ibid., paras. 158-169.

[24] ibid., paras. 170-236.

[25] ILO: *Equal remuneration*, General Survey of the Reports on the Equal Remuneration Convention (No. 100) and Recommendation (No. 90), 1951, Report III (Part 4B), ILC, 72nd Session, 1986, paras. 14-17.

[26] ibid., paras. 19-21; ILO: *Report of the Committee of Experts on the Application of Conventions and Recommendations*, Report III (Part 1A), ILC, 89th Session, 2001, para. 42.

[27] ILO: *Equal remuneration*, General Survey ..., 1986, op. cit., paras. 24-30.

[28] ibid., paras. 138-152; ILO: *Report of the Committee of Experts* ..., Report III (Part 1A), 2001, op. cit., paras. 43 and 44.

[29] ILO: *Equal remuneration*, General Survey ..., 1986, op. cit., para. 31.

[30] ILO: *Equality* ..., Special Survey ..., 1996, op. cit., para. 32.

[31] ILO: *Report of the Committee of Expe*rts ..., Report III (Part 1A), ILC, 90th Session, 2002, op. cit., observations, Convention No. 111, Czech Republic, p. 484, and Latvia, pp. 469-497.

[32] ILO: *Equality* ..., General Survey ..., 1988, op. cit., paras. 47 and 51; ILO: *Equality* ..., Special Survey ..., 1996, op. cit., paras. 41-42.

[33] ILO: *Equality* ..., General Survey ..., 1988, op. cit., paras. 57-60.

[34] ILO: *Equality* ..., Special Survey ..., 1996, op. cit., para. 297.

[35] Particularly seropositivity and HIV status.

[36] ILO: *Equality* ..., Special Survey ..., 1996, op. cit., paras. 206-222.

[37] ILO: *Report of the Committee of Experts* ..., Report III (Part 1A), 2002, op. cit., observation, Convention No. 111, Syrian Arab Republic, para. 512.

[38] ILO: *Equality*..., General Survey ..., 1988, op. cit., paras. 172-184.

[39] ILO: *Report of the Committee of Expe*rts ..., Report III (Part 1A), 2001, op. cit., observation, Convention No. 111, Sudan, pp. 495-496.

[40] ibid., 2002, op. cit., observation, Convention No. 111, Chad, p. 482.

[41] ILO: *Equality* ..., General Survey ..., 1988, op. cit., paras. 185-192.

[42] ILO: *Equality* ..., Special Survey ..., 1996, op. cit., paras. 130-137.

[43] ILO: *Report of the Committee of Experts* ..., Report III (Part 1A), ILC, 87th Session, 1999, pp. 354-355.

Equality of opportunity and treatment

[44] ILO: *Equal remuneration*, General Survey ..., 1986, op. cit., paras. 139-142; ILO: *Report of the Committee of Experts* ..., Report III (Part 1A), 2001, op. cit., paras. 43-44.

[45] ibid., 1999, pp. 354-355.

[46] ILO: *Report of the Committee of Experts* ..., Report III (Part 1A), 2001, op. cit., para. 49.

[47] ILO: *Equality*..., General Survey ..., 1988, op. cit., para. 32.

[48] ibid., paras. 158, 159, 240 and 241.

[49] ILO: *Report of the Committee of Experts* ..., Report III (Part 1A), 2001, op. cit., paras. 45-46.

[50] ibid., para. 40.

PROTECTION OF CHILDREN AND YOUNG PERSONS

Ricardo HERNANDEZ-PULIDO and Tania CARON

6.1 INTRODUCTION

The economic activity of children for their parents in the limited context of economic production in the family unit in pre-industrial societies was considered as the main factor in teaching them their role in society.[1] However, from a source of learning, child labour[2] rapidly turned into exploitation which was harmful to their development. Legal protection therefore became necessary once child labour involved a third party.

At the international level, action to combat the economic exploitation of children began in earnest in 1919 with the creation of the ILO. Up until then, children had been protected against exploitation only at the national level by States which had taken the initiative of adopting legislation to that effect. The protection of children from work and at work is part of the fundamental mandate assigned to the ILO in the Preamble of its Constitution. At the very first session of the International Labour Conference in 1919, the delegates of governments and of employers' and workers' organizations, aware of the need to protect children against economic exploitation, included child labour on the agenda and adopted the Minimum Age (Industry) Convention, 1919 (No. 5). This Convention marks the beginning of the ILO's standard-setting activities to combat child labour. Between 1919 and 1972, the Conference adopted or revised ten Conventions and four Recommendations on the minimum age for admission to employment or work in the various sectors.[3] Moreover, ILO action also covered the conditions of work of children and young persons whose employment was not prohibited by international standards, resulting in the adoption of three Conventions and two Recommendations on the night work of young persons,[4] as well as four Conventions and one Recommendation concerning the medical examination of young persons.[5] The issue of child labour has also been raised by the ILO's supervisory bodies in relation to the application of the Forced Labour Convention, 1930 (No. 29).

Fundamental rights at work and international labour standards

Before 1973, all the ILO instruments on the minimum age for admission to employment or work were essentially intended to address specific sectors, namely industry, maritime work, non-industrial work and underground work. Although this approach allowed member States to ratify only the Conventions that corresponded more fully to their particular situation,[6] it was found that the basic Conventions on minimum age for admission to employment no longer constituted effective instruments of concerted international action to promote the well-being of children.[7] New instruments were therefore needed. In order to enable a greater number of member States to ratify it, the new Convention had to apply to all sectors and be adapted to national situations. It was in that spirit that in 1973 the Conference adopted the Minimum Age Convention (No. 138) and Recommendation (No. 146).

The international community was slow to develop a real system to safeguard the integrity of the child. Even though the 1890 Berlin Conference addressed the issue and certain international instruments refer to children,[8] none of them defines the international legal status of the child. On 20 November 1989, the United Nations General Assembly remedied this situation with the unanimous adoption of the Convention on the Rights of the Child.[9] The adoption of the Convention made a major contribution to the renewal of interest in issues related to the exploitation of children. However, other factors were important, notably greater awareness that the economic exploitation of children may have become worse in many regions of the world as a result of the deterioration in the economic situation and its negative impact on social development, and concern regarding the possibility that certain countries, through the use of the labour of children at ages and under conditions which are not in conformity with ILO standards, would be able to obtain a comparative advantage in relation to other countries which endeavour to apply these standards.

The ILO accompanied this renewal of interest by committing itself more actively to combating child labour, particularly through the launching in 1992 of a large-scale technical cooperation programme called the International Programme for the Elimination of Child Labour (IPEC).[10] The Governing Body then reached the conclusion that existing ILO standards contained a number of shortcomings and that, despite the efforts made, child labour remained a matter of concern, particularly in view of the numbers of children involved, which remained very high.

In June 1996, at its 84th Session, the International Labour Conference adopted a resolution concerning the elimination of child labour. That year, the ILO considered that the time had come for the Conference to adopt new instruments addressing the worst forms of child labour. On 17 June 1999, the 87th Session of the Conference unanimously adopted the Worst Forms of Child Labour Convention (No. 182) and Recommendation (No. 190). The Convention entered into force 15 months after its adoption and has received a considerable number of ratifications, with a large majority of member States having ratified it as of August 2002. This commitment by

Protection of children and young persons

governments has also been beneficial to Convention No. 138, for which the number of ratifications has almost doubled since 1995. This mobilization by governments, and more broadly by the population, bears witness to their will to take action against the economic exploitation of children and achieve lasting protection for childhood.

Moreover, on 18 June 1998, at its 86th Session, the Conference adopted the ILO Declaration on Fundamental Principles and Rights at Work and its Follow-up.[11] The Declaration provides that "all Members, even if they have not ratified the Conventions in question, have an obligation, arising from the very fact of membership in the Organization, to respect, to promote and to realize, in good faith and in accordance with the Constitution, the principles concerning the fundamental rights which are the subject of those Conventions, namely [...] the effective abolition of child labour [...]".

The adoption of standards is one of the means available to the ILO to achieve the objective of social justice set forth in the Preamble to its Constitution. The Conventions and Recommendations adopted by the Conference on the protection of children and young persons form an important part of the ILO's activities in this area. The main elements of the principal standards on child labour are described below, focusing first on the Conventions and Recommendations on the elimination of child labour, followed by those addressing the conditions of work of young persons.

A summary of the relevant ILO instruments is given in tables 6.1 and 6.2 on pp. 116-118.

6.2 THE ELIMINATION OF CHILD LABOUR

6.2.1 Content of the standards

The emphasis placed by international labour standards on the abolition of child labour reflects the conviction of the ILO's constituents that childhood is a period of life which should not be devoted to work, but to the physical and mental development of children, their education, learning their social roles and to games and recreational activities. This conviction is highlighted in both the Minimum Age Convention, 1973 (No. 138), and its corresponding Recommendation (No. 146), and in the Worst Forms of Child Labour Convention, 1999 (No. 182), and the corresponding Recommendation (No. 190).

(a) Determination of a minimum age for admission to employment or work: Convention No. 138 and Recommendation No. 146

The adoption of international labour standards was for a long time the principal means used by the ILO to combat child labour. Over the years, these standards have forged the ILO's doctrine in this respect.[12]

Fundamental rights at work and international labour standards

(i) The evolution of the standards on the minimum age for admission to employment or work

For the ILO, children under a certain age should not engage in an economic activity.[13] In the very year of its creation, the ILO acted on this conviction by adopting the Minimum Age (Industry) Convention, 1919 (No. 5). The nine sectoral Conventions on the minimum age for admission to employment or work which were adopted subsequently (industry, agriculture, trimmers and stokers, maritime work, non-industrial work, fishing and underground work) were based on the same approach.

The first Conventions, those adopted between 1919 and 1932, set[14] the general minimum age for admission to employment or work at 14 years. The Conventions adopted in 1936 and 1937 then set the minimum age for admission to employment or work at 15 years.[15] Other Conventions which cover occupations or activities involving a risk to the health, safety or life of children set stricter standards. For example, the minimum age for admission to employment or work underground was not to be less than 16 years,[16] while that for work performed in high-risk workplaces or those involving a risk of exposure to radiation or hazardous chemical substances was set at 18 years.[17]

These Conventions nevertheless included a number of exceptions.[18] Furthermore, exceptions from the general minimum age for admission to employment or work are permitted by certain Conventions. Others envisage the possibility of determining, under certain conditions, a general minimum age that is either higher or lower, or of determining a lower minimum age for light work. However, all of these instruments were of restrictive scope and only covered limited sectors. The ILO therefore engaged in the revision and regrouping of these standards, resulting in the adoption of Convention No. 138.

(ii) The objective of the 1973 instruments: The effective abolition of child labour and the progressive raising of the minimum age for admission to employment or work

Under Article 1 of Convention No. 138, the primary objective is the pursuit of a "national policy designed to ensure the effective abolition of child labour and to raise progressively the minimum age for admission to employment or work...". The aim pursued is to enable young persons to achieve their fullest physical and mental development. In contrast with the Worst Forms of Child Labour Convention, 1999 (No. 182), Convention No. 138 does not require that measures be taken to abolish child labour within a certain time frame. Indeed, there are graduations in the obligation upon States to pursue a national policy. The development of the policy is conditioned by national circumstances and the level of standards already in force in the country.[19]

Part I of Recommendation No. 146 proposes a framework for action and essential measures which may be implemented to achieve the objectives set out in Article 1 of the Convention. For example, high priority should be given in national development policies and programmes to the measures to be taken to meet the needs of children and youth, and to the progressive extension of the interrelated measures necessary to provide the best possible conditions of physical and mental growth for children and young persons. The following areas should be given special attention in such programmes:

(a) the national commitment to full employment;[20]
(b) economic and social measures to alleviate poverty;
(c) social security and family welfare measures;
(d) education and vocational orientation and training policy; and
(e) the policy for the protection and welfare of children and young persons.

A national policy on child labour is meaningless unless it is coordinated with a policy for childhood. It is therefore necessary to ensure coordination with training, child health and employment policies.[21]

(iii) Scope of application of the 1973 instruments

Convention No. 138 and Recommendation No. 146 are the most recent and complete instruments on the minimum age for admission to employment or work. They revise the ten earlier instruments on minimum age and form a synthesis of the principles set out therein. The earlier instruments are intended to resolve specific problems, without however achieving the aim set forth in the Preamble to Convention No. 138, namely the total abolition of child labour. Convention No. 138 is intended to be "a dynamic instrument" aimed not only at setting a basic standard, but also at its progressive improvement.[22]

Since its creation, the ILO has advocated the elimination of child labour and emphasized that children under a certain age should not engage in a professional occupation. However, its experience has shown that not all forms of work are necessarily harmful to children. Indeed, when appropriately regulated, certain forms of activity may have beneficial effects for the children themselves and for society, particularly where they facilitate the transmission of professional knowledge from one generation to another. This is the underlying reason for a number of the provisions of Convention No. 138 authorizing child labour below the specified minimum age.

Types of employment or work covered

As noted above, the Conventions on minimum age for admission to employment or work developed by the ILO between 1919 and 1973 essentially cover specific sectors, namely industry, agriculture, trimmers and stokers, maritime work, non-industrial work, fishing and underground work. However, Convention No. 138 applies to all sectors, whether or not they employ any children.

It should be emphasized that the terms "employment" and "work" are used together, as in previous Conventions on minimum age, "in order to cover all economic activity regardless of the formal employment status of the person concerned".[23]

Geographical scope

Article 2, paragraph 1, of Convention No. 138 provides that each member State which ratifies the Convention shall specify "a minimum age for admission to employment or work within its territory and on means of transport registered in its territory". This reference to means of transport is intended, in particular, to cover ships. A Member which ratifies the Convention therefore has to regulate the minimum age for admission to employment or work on ships.[24]

(iv) Minimum ages for admission to employment or work

It is more precise to refer to several minimum ages for admission to employment. Convention No. 138 establishes various minimum ages, depending on the types or characteristics of the employment or work performed. It lays down a general minimum age, a higher age for hazardous work and, under certain conditions, a lower age for light work.

Establishment of a general minimum age for admission to employment or work

Article 2, paragraph 1, of Convention No. 138 provides that each Member which ratifies the Convention shall specify a minimum age for admission to employment or work. This provision also lays down that, subject to exceptions permitted by the Convention, "no one under that age shall be admitted to employment or work in any occupation".

The issue of the minimum age for admission to employment is closely related to that of the age at which compulsory schooling ends, in view of the desirability of avoiding any gap between the completion of schooling and admission to work.[25] In accordance with Article 2, paragraph 3, of the Convention, the general minimum age for admission to employment or work shall not be less than the age of completion of compulsory schooling and, in any case, shall not be less than 15 years. Paragraph 4 of Recommendation No. 146 reinforces this principle by indicating that "full-time attendance at school or participation in approved vocational orientation or training programmes should be required and effectively ensured up to an age at least equal to that specified for admission to employment".[26]

Compulsory education is one of the most effective means of combating child labour. Indeed, if the two ages do not coincide, various problems may arise. If compulsory schooling comes to an end before the young persons are legally entitled to work, there may be a period of enforced idleness which may lead to problems such as delinquency.[27] On the other hand, if the age of completion of compulsory schooling is higher than the minimum age for admission to work or employment, then children required to attend school are also legally allowed to work and may thus be encouraged to leave school. Legislation on compulsory education and that on minimum age are mutually reinforcing. Nevertheless, legislation on compulsory school attendance is meaningless if school facilities are inadequate.

Under Article 2, paragraph 4, of the Convention, a Member whose economy and educational facilities are insufficiently developed may initially specify a minimum age of 14 years. In such cases, the organizations of employers and workers concerned must have been consulted beforehand. This flexibility measure must be only an interim stage. Article 2, paragraph 5, of the Convention provides that in the reports submitted to the Office under article 22 of the Constitution, countries must indicate the follow-up to their decision.

Under the terms of Article 2, paragraph 1, of the Convention, member States shall specify a minimum age in a declaration appended to their ratification. Once specified, the minimum age applies to all economic activities, except for the exemptions allowed by the Convention. However, Paragraph 8 of Recommendation No. 146 indicates that, where it is not immediately feasible to fix a minimum age for all employment in agriculture and in related activities in rural areas, a minimum age should be fixed at least for employment on plantations and in the other agricultural enterprises referred to in Article 5, paragraph 3, of the Convention.

Finally, under Article 2, paragraph 2, of Convention No. 138, the general minimum age for admission to employment or work may subsequently be raised. The Member may notify its decision to the Director-General of the ILO by further declarations. In this respect, Paragraph 7(1) of Recommendation No. 146 indicates that "Members should take as their objective the progressive raising to 16 years of the minimum age for admission to employment or work specified in pursuance of Article 2" of Convention No. 138.

Establishment of a higher minimum age for admission to work that is likely to jeopardize health, safety or morals

Article 3, paragraph 1, of Convention No. 138 provides that the minimum age "for admission to any type of employment or work which by its nature or the circumstances in which it is carried out is likely to jeopardise the health, safety or morals of young persons shall not be less than 18 years". Paragraph 9 of Recommendation No. 146 indicates that where the minimum age for admission to hazardous work is below 18 years, immediate steps should be taken to raise it to that level.

Convention No. 138 does not provide any specific definition of hazardous work.[28] Under Article 3, paragraph 2, of the Convention, these types of employment or work shall be determined by national laws or regulations or by the competent authority after consultation with the organizations of employers and workers concerned. Recommendation No. 146 does not give examples of hazardous work either, although in Paragraph 10(1) it indicates that, in determining these types of employment or work, "full account should be taken of relevant international labour standards", such as those concerning dangerous substances, agents or processes, including standards relating to ionizing radiations, the lifting of heavy weights and underground work. In so doing, the Recommendation recognizes the hazardous nature of activities in certain sectors covered by the above international labour standards, which are intended to protect the health and safety of workers. Moreover, in accordance with Paragraph 10(2) of the Recommendation, the list of hazardous types of work should be re-examined periodically, "particularly in the light of advancing scientific and technical knowledge".

Article 3, paragraph 3, of the Convention sets out the conditions under which certain types of employment or work, notwithstanding the provisions of paragraph 1, may be performed as from the age of 16 years. However, the following conditions must be met: (1) the organizations of employers and workers concerned must have been consulted beforehand; (2) the health, safety and morals of the young persons concerned must be fully protected; and (3) they must have received adequate specific instruction or vocational training in the relevant branch of activity.

Night work of children

The Conventions on the night work of young persons are intended to protect them against conditions of work which are prejudicial to their health and development. The principle set out in these Conventions is the prohibition of night work for persons under 18 years of age. However, a number of exceptions are possible.

The Night Work of Young Persons (Industry) Convention, 1919 (No. 6), authorizes night work by young persons over the age of 16 in a limited number of processes that are required to be carried on continuously day and night. The Night Work of Young Persons (Non-Industrial Occupations) Convention, 1946 (No. 79), provides that States may exempt from the general prohibition of night work "... domestic service in private households", and "... employment, on work which is not deemed to be harmful, prejudicial or dangerous to children or young persons, in family undertakings in which only parents and their children or wards are employed". Finally, the Night Work of Young Persons (Industry) Convention (Revised), 1948 (No. 90), envisages the same exceptions as Convention No. 79. It also authorizes night work by young persons aged between 16 and 18 "for purposes of apprenticeship or vocational training in specified industries or occupations which are required to be carried on continuously".

Paragraph 3(e) of the Worst Forms of Child Labour Recommendation, 1999 (No. 190), indicates that "work under particularly difficult conditions", such as the night work of children, should be given consideration as a hazardous form of work to be eliminated as a matter of urgency.

Admission of young persons to certain types of employment or work at a lower age than the general minimum age

In the same way as the earlier instruments,[29] Convention No. 138 provides that, in certain cases and under certain conditions, young children and persons may be authorized to engage in a professional occupation at an age that is lower than the minimum age specified at the time of ratification. The Convention does not provide a definition of "light work".[30] In the absence of a definition, it is the responsibility of the competent authority in each country that ratifies Convention No. 138 to determine the activities to be considered as "light work". Under Article 7, paragraph 1, of the Convention, national laws or regulations may permit the employment or work of persons 13 to 15 years of age on light work which is:

(a) not likely to be harmful to their health or development; and

(b) not such as to prejudice their attendance at school, their participation in vocational orientation or training programmes approved by the competent authority or their capacity to benefit from the instruction received.

Under Article 7, paragraph 2, the employment or work of persons who are at least 15 years of age but have not yet completed their compulsory schooling may be permitted, subject to the above conditions.

Convention No. 138 also contains flexibility clauses in the case of light work. Article 7, paragraph 4, allows a Member which has specified a general minimum age for admission to employment or work of 14 years[31] to substitute the ages of 12 and 14 for the ages of 13 and 15.

Under Article 7, paragraph 3, of the Convention, the competent authority shall determine the activities in which employment or work may be permitted under paragraphs 1 and 2 of the Article. In so doing, the competent authority must prescribe the number of hours during which and the conditions in which such employment or work may be undertaken. Paragraph 13 of Recommendation No. 146 provides details of hours of work and conditions of work and indicates that, in giving effect to Article 7, paragraph 3, of Convention No. 138, special attention should be given to:

- the provision of fair remuneration and its protection, bearing in mind the principle of "equal pay for equal work";
- the strict limitation of the hours spent at work in a day and in a week;
- the prohibition of overtime;
- a minimum consecutive period of 12 hours' night rest;
- an annual holiday with pay of at least four weeks;
- coverage by social security schemes; and
- the maintenance of satisfactory standards of safety and health.

The light work covered by Convention No. 138 is directly related to the conditions under which it is performed (its duration, arduous nature, conditions adapted to the age of the young person, protection of safety and health, etc.) and the schooling of the young persons (attendance and capacity to benefit from the instruction received).

(v) Exceptions

As noted above, Convention No. 138 is general in its scope. It is intended to achieve the objective set out in the Preamble to the Convention, namely "the total abolition of child labour". However, with a view to its adaptation to all national circumstances, the Convention permits a number of exceptions to its application. In addition to the possibility of specifying minimum ages according to the types of employment or work, a Member may exclude from the application of the Convention limited categories of employment or work and certain branches of economic activity. Moreover, it is not bound to apply the Convention to work done by children in educational or training institutions.

Temporary exclusion of limited categories of employment or work

Under Article 4, paragraph 1, of Convention No. 138, it is possible to exclude from the application of the Convention on a temporary basis limited categories of employment or work in respect of which special and substantial problems of application arise. A State that wishes to avail itself of this provision must fulfil the following conditions:

(1) the exclusion of limited categories of employment or work is permitted only in so far as necessary;

(2) the organizations of employers and workers concerned must have been consulted beforehand; and

(3) the limited categories of employment which have been excluded must be listed, giving the reasons for such exclusion, in the first report that the State has to submit on the application of the Convention under article 22 of the Constitution of the ILO.

Subsequent reports must indicate developments in the position of the country's law and practice in respect of these categories.

With a view to leaving a certain latitude to each country to adapt the application of the Convention to its national situation, the Convention does not enumerate the categories of employment or work which may be covered by such an exclusion. However, examples might include employment in family enterprises, domestic service in private households, and home work or other work outside the supervision and control of the employer, including young persons working on their own account.[32] These illustrations are not restrictive.

It is important to recall that Article 4, paragraph 3, of Convention No. 138 does not permit the exclusion from its application of dangerous work.[33]

Protection of children and young persons

Limitation of the scope of the Convention

Article 5, paragraph 1, of the Convention permits a Member whose economy and administrative facilities are insufficiently developed to initially limit the scope of application of the Convention. A Member which wishes to avail itself of this provision must fulfil the following conditions:

(1) consult the organizations of employers and workers concerned;[34]

(2) specify, in a declaration appended to its ratification, the branches of economic activity or types of enterprises to which it will apply the provisions of the Convention;[35] and

(3) indicate, in the reports that it has to submit under article 22 of the Constitution of the ILO, the general position as regards the employment or work of young persons and children in the branches of activity which are excluded from the scope of application of the Convention, and any progress which may have been made towards wider application of the provisions of the Convention.[36]

As the Committee of Experts has emphasized on a number of occasions, this flexibility clause must be used at the time of ratification and cannot be invoked subsequently. Under Article 5, paragraph 4(b), a Member may at any time extend the scope of application of the Convention by a declaration addressed to the Director-General of the ILO.

Nevertheless, Article 5, paragraph 3, lists seven sectors which must as a minimum be covered by the Convention: mining and quarrying; manufacturing; construction; electricity; gas and water; sanitary services; and transport, storage and communication, as well as plantations and other agricultural enterprises producing mainly for commercial purposes, but excluding family and small-scale holdings producing for local consumption and not regularly employing hired workers.

A distinction should be made between the provisions of Article 5 and those of Article 4 reviewed above. While Article 5 permits the exclusion of an entire economic sector, Article 4 allows exceptions for limited categories of employment or work, and thereby permits the exemption of a profession.

Work done by children and young persons in general, vocational or technical education

Article 6 of Convention No. 138 addresses two aspects. Firstly, it provides that the Convention does not apply to "work done by children and young persons in schools for general, vocational or technical education or in other training institutions".[37] Secondly, it lays down that the Convention does not apply to work done by persons at least 14 years of age in enterprises where such work is carried out in accordance with conditions prescribed by the competent authority, after consultation with the organizations of employers and workers concerned, and where it is an integral part of:

(a) a course of education or training for which a school or training institution is primarily responsible;

(b) a programme of training mainly or entirely in an enterprise, where the programme has been approved by the competent authority; or

(c) a programme of guidance or orientation designed to facilitate the choice of an occupation or of a line of training.

This latter provision, without using the term, is intended to cover apprenticeship.

Under Paragraph 12(2) of Recommendation No. 146, measures should also be taken to safeguard and supervise the conditions in which children and young persons undergo vocational orientation and training and to formulate standards for their protection and development.

Artistic performances

Article 8 of Convention No. 138 authorizes the participation of children who have not attained the general minimum age for admission to employment or work in activities such as artistic performances. In contrast with certain earlier Conventions,[38] Convention No. 138 is less restrictive in the conditions it sets for such authorization. It requires that:

(1) permits must be granted in individual cases;

(2) the organizations of employers and workers concerned must be consulted beforehand; and

(3) the permits must limit the number of hours during which, and prescribe the conditions in which, employment or work is allowed.

National legislation cannot provide for general exceptions. Convention No. 138 is therefore intended to ensure strict supervision of the circumstances and conditions under which young persons participate in artistic performances.[39] It should be noted that the Convention does not lay down a minimum age for the participation of children in this type of activity.

(vi) Conditions of work of children

Convention No. 138 contains very few provisions relating to the conditions of work of young people. When it mentions them, it does so in a specific context. For example, Article 7, paragraph 3, provides that the competent authority shall prescribe the number of hours during which and the conditions in which light work may be undertaken, including by persons who are at least 15 years of age but have not yet completed their compulsory schooling. Article 8, paragraph 2, provides that permits granted for participation in such activities as artistic performances "shall limit the number of hours during which and prescribe the conditions in which employment or work is allowed". These provisions are examined below in the relevant sections.

Protection of children and young persons

The Convention does not contain explicit standards relating to the conditions which must be applied to young persons and children performing an occupational activity other than in these special circumstances. Nevertheless, it should be emphasized that most international labour standards apply without distinction on grounds of age. They therefore apply to children who are engaged in work in the same way as to adults, irrespective of their sex.[40]

These issues are covered by Recommendation No. 146 in Paragraphs 12 and 13. Paragraph 12 indicates that the conditions in which children and young persons under the age of 18 years are employed or work should be specified and supervised. The same applies to the conditions in which children and young persons undergo vocational orientation and training. Furthermore, Paragraph 13 of the Recommendation contains a list of points relating to conditions of employment to which special attention should be given:

- the provision of fair remuneration and its protection, bearing in mind the principle of "equal pay for equal work";
- the strict limitation of the hours spent at work in a day and in a week, and the prohibition of overtime, so as to allow enough time for education and training (including the time needed for related homework), for rest during the day and for leisure activities;
- the granting, without possibility of exception save in genuine emergency, of a minimum consecutive period of 12 hours' night rest;[41]
- the granting of an annual holiday with pay of at least four weeks and, in any case, not shorter than that granted to adults;
- coverage by social security schemes, whatever the conditions of employment or work may be; and
- the maintenance of satisfactory standards of safety and health and appropriate instruction and supervision.

(vii) Application of the standards

The ratification of a Convention by a member State is an expression of its political will to take action and gives rise to obligations for that State. In particular, these include the substantive obligation for the State to give full effect to the Convention in law and in practice.[42] Convention No. 138 is no exception.

Necessary measures and appropriate penalties

Under the terms of Article 9, paragraph 1, of Convention No. 138, the competent authority must take all necessary measures, including the provision of appropriate penalties, to ensure the effective enforcement of the provisions of the Convention. The necessary measures may take several forms. For example, they may consist of the adoption of national legislation on child labour or the development of a national policy.[43] The strengthening of labour inspection services is also essential for the effective implementation of the Convention. As indicated in Paragraph 14 of Recommendation No. 146, such strengthening may be achieved, for example, by the special training of inspectors to detect abuses in the employment or work of children and young persons. It should also be noted that Paragraph 14 of the Recommendation emphasizes the important role played by inspection services in the application of national legislation respecting child labour.[44] Programmes to inform and raise awareness of persons who are regularly in contact with children, as well as the population in general, concerning the forms and effects of child labour are also a means of giving effect to the Convention. Reference may be made, for example, to parents and children themselves, employers, organizations of employers and teachers.

The adoption of national legislation is essential as it establishes a framework within which society determines its responsibilities with regard to young persons. However, the best legislation only takes on real value when it is applied. For this purpose, the Convention also provides that penalties have to be adopted. However, it does not indicate the types of penalties and confines itself to indicating that they have to be "appropriate" and designed to ensure "the effective enforcement" of the provisions of the Convention. They may consist of fines or sentences of imprisonment. In general terms, in terms of the application of labour law, it may be said that although sanctions are indispensable, they do not suffice in themselves to ensure the application of labour legislation.

Determination of the persons responsible for compliance with the Convention

Article 9, paragraph 2, of Convention No. 138 provides that national laws or regulations or the competent authority shall define the persons responsible for compliance with the provisions giving effect to the Convention. It should be noted that "the persons responsible for compliance" with the provisions are not the governmental bodies enforcing the provisions of the Conventions, but those against whom they are enforced.[45] These persons may be employers, parents or other persons required to respect legal provisions.

Maintenance of registers

In accordance with Article 9, paragraph 3, of Convention No. 138, the employer has to keep and make available registers or other documents. These registers or documents must contain the names and ages or dates of birth of persons who are less than 18 years of age and who are employed or work for the employer. Paragraph 16(a) and (b) of Recommendation No. 146 indicates the measures which should be taken to facilitate the verification of the ages of the persons concerned. The Recommendation suggests the maintenance of an effective system of birth registration and the keeping by employers of registers containing information not only on children and young persons employed by them, but also on those receiving vocational orientation or training.

With regard to the form of the required registers, the terms of the Convention leave broad latitude to member States to determine the manner in which effect is given to these requirements.[46]

(viii) Implementation of the instruments under examination: Problems and challenges

The abolition of child labour is first and foremost a national responsibility. Practice shows that collaboration with organizations of employers and workers, non-governmental organizations, local communities and other associations is essential for a strategy to combat the economic exploitation of children. However, without the commitment and political will of governments, it is difficult to combat this scourge. Indeed, both the Constitution of the ILO and the provisions of the various Conventions leave great latitude to member States in their implementation. Moreover, in addition to the substantive obligation of member States, there is also a formal obligation, as set out in article 22 of the Constitution of the ILO, by virtue of which member States must provide reports on the application of ratified Conventions. On the basis of these reports, the Committee of Experts endeavours to establish a constructive dialogue with member States with a view to the full application of the Convention.

National policy

In its general observation of 1996, the Committee of Experts recalled that member States ratifying Convention No. 138 undertake to pursue a national policy designed to ensure the effective abolition of child labour and to raise progressively the minimum age for admission to employment or work. Since then, a number of member States have adopted a national policy to that effect.

Establishment of a general minimum age for admission to employment or work

Almost all countries have adopted laws and regulations to prohibit the employment of children who have not reached a certain age. However, a large number of countries set the minimum age for admission to employment or work for specific sectors of activity. One of the issues raised most frequently by the Committee of Experts therefore concerns the scope of such legislation. On several occasions, the Committee has reminded governments that the Convention applies to all sectors of economic activity and that it covers all forms of employment or work, whether or not there is a contract of employment and regardless of whether or not the work is remunerated. The Committee of Experts has also emphasized that own-account work is covered by the Convention.

Fundamental rights at work and international labour standards

Examination of national legislation shows that certain member States have raised the minimum age that they declared when ratifying the Convention. On a number of occasions, the Committee of Experts has therefore drawn the attention of governments to the possibility afforded by the Convention to inform the Director-General of the ILO, in a declaration, that they have raised the minimum age specified at the time of ratification.

In contrast, certain member States adopt legislation lowering the minimum age specified at the time of ratification. The Committee of Experts has therefore indicated to the governments concerned that once the minimum age for admission to employment or work has been specified and indicated in the declaration appended to the instrument of ratification, it can no longer be lowered.

Dangerous work

The great majority of countries have adopted laws and regulations prohibiting work that is dangerous for children. However, some have not specified the age for admission to such work, or have set an age that is lower than that authorized by the Convention, namely 18 years. On several occasions, the Committee of Experts has therefore requested the governments concerned to take the necessary measures to set the age for admission to dangerous work at 18 years and, when this age has been specified, to ensure that young persons under 18 years of age are not employed in such activities.

In cases in which children of at least 16 years of age are permitted to perform dangerous work, the Committee of Experts has recalled that the Convention only authorizes this under strict conditions. Another difficulty arising in the application of the Convention concerns the determination by laws and regulations of the types of employment or work considered to be dangerous. The legislation sometimes sets out in detail the types of work that are dangerous, and sometimes defines dangerous work according to the general terms of the Convention. The Committee of Experts has recalled that it is indispensable to determine, at the national level, the nature of the work and the types of employment or work which are prohibited for young persons under 18 years of age.

Convention No. 138 provides that dangerous work must be determined after consultation with the organizations of employers and workers concerned. On many occasions, the Committee of Experts has emphasized this essential provision.

Light work

The Committee of Experts has often addressed the issue of light work jointly with that of the determination of the general minimum age for admission to employment. Indeed, in several countries, the legislation allows children under the age of 15 to work, without determining the types of work that they may perform. The Committee of Experts has therefore reminded the countries concerned that admission to light work is only possible under

Protection of children and young persons

the conditions set out in Article 7 of the Convention and for persons between 13 and 15 years of age.[47] On several occasions, the Committee has also emphasized that the competent authority must determine the activities in which such employment or work can be authorized, the number of hours and the conditions of work.

Artistic performances

Certain countries have adopted legal provisions concerning artistic performances. However, the conditions for the implementation of Article 8 are not always met. In certain cases, the Committee of Experts has therefore recalled that an exception to Article 2 concerning the prohibition of employment or work before reaching the minimum age for admission to employment or work, which is to be specified when ratifying the Convention, for the purposes of participation in artistic performances is only allowed when the competent authority issues an individual permit specifying the conditions governing the employment or work. Furthermore, the Committee of Experts has emphasized that prior consultation of the organizations of employers and workers is required.

Labour inspection and child labour

In 2000, the Committee of Experts made a general observation concerning the Labour Inspection Convention, 1947 (No. 81). The observation directly addressed the issue of labour inspection and child labour. In this respect, the Committee of Experts noted that the government reports and annual reports on the work of the inspection services which are communicated to the ILO contain an increasing volume of detailed information on the matters covered by the Convention, including those related to the protection of the fundamental rights of workers. The Committee of Experts also noted that cooperation between the inspection services and the various bodies and institutions concerned, as well as collaboration with employers' and workers' organizations, has made it possible in a large number of countries to establish effective systems for the communication of information in many fields related to the protection of workers while engaged in their work. However, the Committee of Experts regretted that information was seldom provided by governments in their reports or by the central authority in the annual reports on the work of the inspection services concerning the supervisory and advisory work relating to child labour. The Committee of Experts therefore requested governments to take appropriate measures to ensure that supervising the application of legal provisions on child labour become one of the priorities of the labour inspection services and that information on this matter be regularly included in the annual reports to be submitted under article 22 of the Constitution.

(b) The prohibition and elimination of the worst forms of child labour: Convention No. 182 and Recommendation No. 190

As noted above, since the beginning of the 1990s, the international community has been showing growing interest in the issue of the rights of the child. However, despite the efforts made, child labour is an increasingly serious problem in many countries. Therefore, following the discussions on child labour held in 1995 and 1996,[48] the Governing Body decided to include this issue on the agenda of the International Labour Conference in 1998 with a view to the adoption of new instruments.[49] These discussions identified a number of shortcomings in the existing instruments. There was therefore broad consensus on the need to launch new concerted action to combat child labour. The origins of the new instruments lie in the need to remedy these shortcomings and to respond to the will of constituents to take action.[50] The objective is to strengthen ILO standards with a binding instrument focusing on the worst forms of child labour.

Following the discussions in the Committee on Child Labour at the Conference in 1998 and 1999, the Worst Forms of Child Labour Convention (No. 182), and Recommendation (No. 190), were adopted unanimously on 17 June 1999.

(i) Objective of the 1999 instruments

Convention No. 182 is based on Convention No. 138, which is one of the ILO's fundamental Conventions and the key instrument for the development of a coherent strategy to combat child labour at the national level.[51] The Preamble to Convention No. 182 indicates, inter alia, that it is necessary "to adopt new instruments for the prohibition and elimination of the worst forms of child labour, as the main priority for national and international action [...] to complement the Convention and the Recommendation concerning Minimum Age for Admission to Employment, 1973 [...]".

Convention No. 182 sets forth the principle that certain forms of child labour cannot be tolerated and therefore cannot be subject to progressive elimination.[52] Under Article 1 of the Convention, each "Member which ratifies this Convention shall take immediate and effective measures to secure the prohibition and elimination of the worst forms of child labour as a matter of urgency". With regard to the term "immediate", the Office has emphasized that it has the meaning of "done at once or without delay". Proceeding immediately therefore implies taking immediate measures without waiting for progress on achieving longer-term goals.[53]

Under the terms of Article 1 of Convention No. 182, the measures taken must ensure not only the prohibition, but also the elimination of the worst forms of child labour. For the effective elimination of child labour, both immediate action and time-bound measures would therefore seem to be necessary.[54] In this respect, Article 1 has to be read in conjunction with Article 7, paragraph 2, of Convention No. 182.

(ii) Definition of "child"

Under Article 2 of Convention No. 182, "the term 'child' shall apply to all persons under the age of 18", and therefore includes children, adolescents and young persons. The age of 18 years corresponds to the higher age limit set out in Convention No. 138 for work which is likely to jeopardize the health, safety or morals of young persons, as well as the general definition of the child contained in Article 1 of the Convention on the Rights of the Child. It does not therefore have any impact on the lower age limits for admission to employment or work which are authorized by Convention No. 138.[55]

(iii) The worst forms of child labour

As indicated above, Convention No. 182 places emphasis on the worst forms of child labour and obliges States ratifying the Convention to take priority measures in the form of immediate action. It is based in part on Convention No. 138 and, to a lesser extent, on Convention No. 29.[56] Convention No. 182 enumerates in detail the types of work which are prohibited for children under the age of 18. The definition of the "worst forms of child labour" is therefore fundamental to an understanding of the scope of the new instruments.

As will be seen below, the worst forms of child labour include all forms of slavery or practices similar to slavery, prostitution and the production of pornography or pornographic performances, and illicit activities. It is important to note that the ILO's concern with these practices is that, "while they are crimes they are also forms of economic exploitation akin to forced labour and slavery".[57]

All forms of slavery or practices similar to slavery

Under Article 3(a) of Convention No. 182, the term "the worst forms of child labour" comprises, inter alia, "all forms of slavery or practices similar to slavery, such as the sale and trafficking of children, debt bondage and serfdom and forced or compulsory labour".

In view of the fact that Convention No. 182 does not provide any definition of forced labour, the definition contained in Article 2 of Convention No. 29 remains valid for the purposes of Convention No. 182.[58] With regard to debt bondage and serfdom, it is necessary to refer to the instruments of the United Nations[59] for a definition, as Convention No. 29 does not contain one. The expression "the sale and trafficking of children" is not meant to cover issues unrelated to the worst forms of child labour, such as adoption.[60]

In reply to a Government member who raised the question of the implications of this provision "for member States which allowed compulsory military service as of the age of 17", the Legal Adviser explained that "the purpose of the proposal on Article 3(a) was to cover forced or compulsory recruitment of children for use in armed conflict".[61]

Prostitution, the production of pornography or pornographic performances

Under Article 3(b) of Convention No. 182, the term "the worst forms of child labour" also comprises "the use, procuring or offering of a child for prostitution, for the production of pornography or for pornographic performances". It should be noted that Article 3(b) of Convention No. 182 does not provide a definition, in view of the existence of relevant international instruments.[62] In this regard, the Office emphasized that "where there are no internationally accepted definitions, national definitions apply".[63]

Finally, it should be recalled that procuring or offering a child, which may also occur over the Internet, is covered by this provision of the Convention. The medium of dissemination and consumption of the material produced using children is not directly addressed, and is thus left to the national legislator. However, the existence of pornographic material on the Internet would constitute proof of violation of the prohibition against using children to produce such material.[64]

Illicit activities

Under Article 3(c) of Convention No. 182, the term "the worst forms of child labour" comprises "the use, procuring or offering of a child for illicit activities". Examples of such illicit activities include the use, procuring or offering of a child for the production and trafficking of drugs. Convention No. 182 does not provide a definition of the drugs to which this provision refers. However, subparagraph (c) makes reference to "the relevant international treaties".[65]

Hazardous work

Under Article 3(d) of Convention No. 182, "work which, by its nature or the circumstances in which it is carried out, is likely to harm the health, safety or morals of children" is also considered to be one of the worst forms of child labour. The types of work covered by subparagraph (d) are those considered to be particularly hazardous and which must therefore be prohibited and eliminated in all sectors, in accordance with the objective, which is to prohibit types of work which are intolerable in all countries, irrespective of their level of development.[66]

Paragraph 3 of Recommendation No. 190 establishes a list of activities or types of work to which consideration should be given when such types of hazardous work are being determined. This list includes:

- work which exposes children to physical, psychological or sexual abuse;
- work underground, under water, at dangerous heights or in confined spaces;
- work with dangerous machinery, equipment and tools, or which involves the manual handling or transport of heavy loads;

- work in an unhealthy environment which may, for example, expose children to hazardous substances, agents or processes, or to temperatures, noise levels, or vibrations damaging to their health;
- work under particularly difficult conditions such as work for long hours or during the night, or work where the child is unreasonably confined to the premises of the employer.

Further to this list, it should be emphasized that Article 4, paragraph 1, of Convention No. 182 provides that, when determining the types of work referred to under Article 3(d), consideration must be given to "relevant international standards". This reference does not oblige governments to comply with the provisions of instruments that they have not ratified,[67] or which are not by their nature ratifiable.[68] They consist of standards which can aid in the determination of what is likely to jeopardize the health, safety or morals of children. The obligation in this respect is one of procedure: to examine in good faith whether the types of work covered by these instruments should or should not, in a country covered by the Convention, be considered as "the worst forms of child labour" within the meaning of Article 3(d) of the Convention. The types of work to be determined may be activities or occupations.[69]

In the absence of a precise definition of hazardous work, as indicated in the instruments on minimum age, it is therefore left to national laws or regulations to determine hazardous types of work, based on the examples provided in these instruments and the relevant international standards. In the same way as Convention No. 138, Article 4, paragraph 2, of Convention No. 182 adds the obligation of consultation with the organizations of employers and workers concerned when identifying the types of work covered by Article 3(d). However, Article 4, paragraph 2, of Convention No. 182 is more detailed than the corresponding provision in Convention No. 138, since it requires the competent authority to identify where hazardous types of work so determined exist.

Reference should be made to the differences in the wording of the two instruments. Article 3 of Convention No. 138 refers to "any type of employment or work which by its nature or the circumstances in which it is carried out is likely to jeopardise the health, safety or morals of young persons"; while Article 3(d) of Convention No. 182 refers to "work which, by its nature or the circumstances in which it is carried out, is likely to harm the health, safety or morals of children". The principal difference is that the wording of Convention No. 138 covers a larger number of situations than Convention No. 182. It may logically be deduced that the types of hazardous work covered by Convention No. 182 are less numerous than those referred to by Convention No. 138. The list envisaged by Article 4 of Convention No. 182 should therefore only contain the "worst forms" of hazardous work and, in any case, those which are likely to "harm", and not only "jeopardize", the health, safety or morals of children.

(iv) Effective implementation of the standards

Under Article 5 of Convention No. 182, each Member which ratifies the Convention shall establish or designate appropriate mechanisms to monitor the implementation of its provisions. These mechanisms must be determined after consultation with employers' and workers' organizations.

With regard to the terms "appropriate mechanisms", the Legal Adviser of the ILO indicated that "the draft instruments did not define the nature of the mechanisms but required the establishment or designation of a national mechanism".[70] With regard to the term "monitoring", the Office recalled that it has the sense of "overseeing implementation, and the monitoring body could involve representation from civil society". The committees set up under the United Nations Convention on the Rights of the Child or national committees or advisory bodies on child labour were mentioned as examples by certain countries. "The United Nations Committee on the Rights of the Child suggests that the reference be to a multidisciplinary mechanism."[71]

Paragraph 8 of Recommendation No. 190 indicates that Members should establish or designate appropriate national mechanisms to monitor the implementation of national provisions for the prohibition and elimination of the worst forms of child labour. It also indicates that such designation should be made after consultation with employers' and workers' organizations.

In accordance with Article 6 of Convention No. 182, governments are under the obligation to "design and implement programmes of action to eliminate as a priority the worst forms of child labour". Moreover, such "programmes of action shall be designed and implemented in consultation with relevant government institutions and employers' and workers' organizations, taking into consideration the views of other concerned groups as appropriate".

With regard to the term "other concerned groups", neither Convention No. 182 nor Recommendation No. 190 gives a precise definition. However, these could "for example, be parents' organizations, children's associations or organizations for the defence of children". Article 6, paragraph 2, takes into account the tripartite role of the constituents and accords them priority in the consultation process.[72]

Moreover, Paragraph 2 of Recommendation No. 190 indicates that the programmes of action referred to in Article 6 of the Convention should be designed and implemented as a matter of urgency. The relevant government institutions and employers' and workers' organizations should be consulted, and the views of the children directly affected by the worst forms of child labour, their families and, as appropriate, other concerned groups committed to the aims of the Convention and the Recommendation, should be taken into consideration. The programmes should aim at, inter alia: identifying and denouncing the worst forms of child labour; preventing the engagement of children in or removing them from the worst forms of child labour;

Protection of children and young persons

giving special attention to younger children and the girl child; identifying, reaching out to and working with communities where children are at special risk; and informing, sensitizing and mobilizing public opinion and concerned groups.

Article 7, paragraph 1, of Convention No. 182 provides that member States which ratify the Convention shall "take all necessary measures to ensure the effective implementation and enforcement of the provisions [...] including the provision and application of penal sanctions or, as appropriate, other sanctions". The objective is for sanctions to be imposed, which may be penal or of any other nature as appropriate.[73] The Convention does not indicate the types of sanctions. As noted in the case of Convention No. 138, the necessary measures may take several forms. Fines, sentences of imprisonment, temporary or permanent prohibition from exercising a specific activity, or damages with interest are illustrations of the types of sanctions which may be taken by a member State.

Paragraph 12 of Recommendation No. 190 indicates that Members should provide that all forms of slavery or practices similar to slavery, prostitution or the production of pornography or pornographic performances, and the use, procuring or offering of a child for illicit activities, as set out in Convention No. 182, are criminal offences. Paragraph 13 of the Recommendation suggests that penalties including, where appropriate, criminal penalties should be applied for violations of the national provisions on the prohibition and elimination of any type of hazardous work referred to in Article 3(d) of Convention No. 182.

Under Article 7, paragraph 2, of Convention No. 182, each Member "shall, taking into account the importance of education in eliminating child labour, take effective and time-bound measures to":

- prevent the engagement of children in the worst forms of child labour;
- provide the necessary and appropriate direct assistance for the removal of children from the worst forms of child labour, and for their rehabilitation and social integration;
- ensure access to free basic education, and, wherever possible and appropriate, vocational training, for all children removed from the worst forms of child labour;
- identify and reach out to children at special risk; and
- take account of the special situation of girls.

It is important to specify the meaning of the phrase "take effective and time-bound measures". As noted above,[74] to proceed immediately implies taking immediate measures without waiting for progress on achieving longer-term goals. However, effective elimination would seem to require both immediate and time-bound measures. Immediate measures could include, for instance, removal from intolerable situations. For example, as soon as children are found in bondage, in a brothel or deep in a mine, it is necessary to take action and emergency measures are required until assistance and rehabilitation can be provided to them. Other measures could then be taken, for example with a view to prevention, which could require a certain time frame for implementation and should be time-bound. Prevention, rehabilitation and social reintegration, as called for in Article 7, could give rise to immediate and time-bound action.[75]

Finally, Article 8 of the Convention provides that member States which ratify it shall take appropriate steps to assist one another in giving effect to the provisions of the Convention "through enhanced international cooperation and/or assistance including support for social and economic development, poverty eradication programmes and universal education". With regard to the obligation for member States "to assist one another", the Legal Adviser of the ILO, in response to a question raised by a Government member of the Conference Committee, "stressed the idea of partnership contained in the spirit of the Article". He emphasized that "no obligation would arise from either proposal for ratifying member States in relation to a particular level or form of cooperation or assistance. There was only an obligation to take appropriate steps towards enhanced international partnerships, and it was up to individual States to decide on those appropriate steps."[76] A Government member of the Conference Committee, referring to the comments of the Legal Adviser, indicated that the term "partnerships" used by the Legal Adviser meant "working together" and that Article 8 encouraged member States to work together to meet the goals of the Convention.[77]

Paragraphs 11 and 16 of Recommendation No. 190 provide indications on the manner in which member States could cooperate and/or assist in international efforts to prohibit and eliminate the worst forms of child labour. For this purpose, they could: gather and exchange information concerning criminal offences, including those involving international networks; detect and prosecute those involved in the sale and trafficking of children, or in the use, procuring or offering of children for illicit activities, for prostitution, for the production of pornography or for pornographic performances; and register perpetrators of such offences. Such international cooperation and/or assistance should include: mobilizing resources for national and international programmes; mutual legal assistance; technical assistance including the exchange of information; and support for social and economic development, poverty eradication programmes and universal education.

6.3 CONDITIONS OF EMPLOYMENT OF YOUNG PERSONS

6.3.1 Content of the standards

Certain ILO Conventions provide that in specific sectors, before being admitted to employment, young persons must undergo a medical examination for fitness for employment with a view to limiting the risks inherent in the work that they are to perform. They set a minimum age up to which it is compulsory for a young person to undergo such an examination and provide for regular medical examinations up to a certain age.

(a) The Medical Examination of Young Persons (Industry) Convention, 1946 (No. 77), and the Medical Examination of Young Persons (Non-Industrial Occupations) Convention, 1946 (No. 78)

(i) Scope of application of Conventions Nos. 77 and 78

Convention No. 77 applies to children and young persons employed or working in, or in connection with, industrial enterprises, whether public or private.[78] For the purposes of the Convention, industrial enterprises are considered to include: mines, quarries and other works for the extraction of minerals from the earth; enterprises in which articles are manufactured, altered, cleaned, repaired, ornamented, finished, adapted for sale, broken up or demolished, or in which materials are transformed, including enterprises engaged in shipbuilding or in the generation, transformation or transmission of electricity or motive power of any kind; enterprises engaged in building or civil engineering work, including constructional, repair, maintenance, alteration and demolition work; and enterprises engaged in the transport of passengers or goods by road, rail, inland waterway or air, including the handling of goods at docks, quays, wharves, warehouses or airports.

Convention No. 78 applies to children and young persons employed for wages, or working directly or indirectly for gain, in non-industrial occupations, which mean all occupations other than those recognized by the competent authority as industrial, agricultural or maritime occupations.[79] Convention No. 78 envisages the possibility of exempting from its application work which is recognized as not being dangerous to the health of children or young persons in family enterprises in which only parents and their children or wards are employed.[80]

(ii) Medical examination

Although they apply to different sectors, Conventions Nos. 77 and 78 contain analogous provisions which make it compulsory for young persons to undergo a medical examination for fitness for employment before they are admitted to employment.

Thorough medical examination

Conventions No. 77 and 78 provide that children and young persons under 18 years of age shall not be admitted to employment by an industrial enterprise or in non-industrial occupations unless they have been found fit for the work on which they are to be employed by a thorough medical examination.[81] The medical examination for fitness for employment has to be carried out by a qualified physician approved by the competent authority and certified either by a medical certificate or by an endorsement on the work permit or in the workbook.[82] In occupations which involve high health risks, the medical examination for fitness for employment shall be required until at least the age of 21 years.[83]

The medical examination shall not involve the child or young person, or his or her parents, in any expense.[84]

Repetition of medical examinations

The fitness of children or young persons for the employment in which they are engaged shall be subject to medical supervision until they have attained the age of 18 years.[85] The continued employment of children or young persons under 18 years of age shall be subject to the repetition of medical examinations at intervals of not more than one year.[86] In the same way as for the medical examination for fitness for employment, in occupations which involve high health risks, periodical medical re-examinations have to be required until at least the age of 21 years.[87]

With regard to medical re-examinations, national laws or regulations shall make provision for the special circumstances in which a medical re-examination shall be required, in addition to the annual examination or at more frequent intervals, in order to ensure effective supervision in respect of the risks involved in the occupation and of the state of health of the child or young person as shown by previous examinations; or empower the competent authority to require medical re-examinations in exceptional cases.[88]

(iii) Implementation of the instruments under examination

As already mentioned, Conventions Nos. 77 and 78 contain a number of identical provisions; the scope of application of these provisions is different, however, since Convention No. 77 applies to industrial work and Convention No. 78 to non-industrial occupations. Reference is made below firstly to the comments of the Committee of Experts on the provisions of the Conventions which are identical, and then on certain aspects which are related to each Convention specifically.

Identical provisions of Conventions Nos. 77 and 78

Medical examination for fitness for employment for children and young persons under 18 years of age

In most cases, the Committee of Experts has reminded governments that the medical examination for fitness for employment is obligatory for

Protection of children and young persons

children and young persons under 18 years of age. In addition, it has emphasized that the fitness of children and young persons must be determined by means of medical examinations until the age of 18.

It has also drawn the attention of governments to the fact that the medical examination must be thorough and go beyond the issuing of a mere certificate of good health.

*Medical examination for fitness for employment
up to the age of 21 years*

The Committee of Experts has frequently emphasized that, in occupations involving high health risks, medical examinations for fitness for employment and re-examinations must be carried out up to the age of 21 years. Moreover, it has recalled that the occupations and categories of occupations in which medical examinations for fitness for employment are required until at least the age of 21 years have to be specified by national laws or regulations.

*Provision of medical examinations
free of charge*

In certain cases, the Committee of Experts has emphasized that the medical examinations required by Conventions Nos. 77 and 78 must not involve any expense for the children or young persons, or their parents.

*Measures for vocational guidance
and physical and vocational rehabilitation*

On several occasions, the Committee of Experts has recalled that appropriate measures have to be taken for the vocational guidance and physical and vocational rehabilitation of children and young persons found by medical examination to be unsuited to certain types of work or to have physical handicaps or limitations.

Provisions related to specific Conventions
Convention No. 77

In contrast with Convention No. 78, no exceptions from its provisions are envisaged by Convention No. 77. In certain cases, the Committee of Experts has therefore recalled that the Convention applies to all industrial enterprises, irrespective of the number of workers that they employ.

Convention No. 78

Employment covered by the Convention. In certain cases, the Committee of Experts has emphasized that, apart from the possibilities of exempting from the application of the Convention employment in family enterprises in which only parents and their children or wards are occupied on work which is recognized as not being dangerous to the health of children or young persons, no other employment may be excluded.

Fundamental rights at work and international labour standards

Table 6.1 Instruments on the elimination of child labour

Instruments	Number of ratifications (31 August 2002)	Status
Up-to-date instruments (Conventions whose ratification is encouraged and Recommendations to which member States are invited to give effect.)		
Minimum Age Convention, 1973 (No. 138)	117	Fundamental Convention.
Minimum Age Recommendation, 1973 (No. 146)	–	This Recommendation is related to a fundamental Convention and is considered up to date.
Worst Forms of Child Labour Convention, 1999 (No. 182)	129	Fundamental Convention.
Worst Forms of Child Labour Recommendation, 1999 (No. 190)	–	This Recommendation is related to a fundamental Convention and is considered up to date.
Other instruments (This category comprises instruments that are no longer fully up to date but remain relevant in certain respects.)		
Minimum Age (Non-Industrial Employment) Recommendation, 1932 (No. 41)	–	The Governing Body has decided to maintain the status quo with regard to Recommendations Nos. 41 and 52.
Minimum Age (Family Undertakings) Recommendation, 1937 (No. 52)	–	
Outdated instruments (Instruments that are no longer up to date; this category includes the Conventions that member States are no longer invited to ratify and the Recommendations whose implementation is no longer encouraged.)		
Minimum Age (Industry) Convention, 1919 (No. 5)	20	The Governing Body has invited the States parties to Convention No. 5 to contemplate ratifying the Minimum Age Convention, 1973 (No. 138), and denouncing Convention No. 5 at the same time, with recourse to technical assistance as required.
Minimum Age (Agriculture) Convention, 1921 (No. 10)	13	The Governing Body has invited States parties to Convention No. 10 to contemplate ratifying the Minimum Age Convention, 1973 (No. 138), which would involve the denunciation of Convention No. 10 on the condition stated in Article 10(5)(b) of Convention No. 138, with recourse to technical assistance as required.
Minimum Age (Non-Industrial Employment) Convention, 1932 (No. 33)	8	The Governing Body has invited States parties to Convention No. 33 to contemplate ratifying the Minimum Age Convention, 1973 (No. 138), which would *ipso jure* involve the immediate denunciation of Convention No. 33 on the condition stated in Article 10(4)(b) of Convention No. 138, with recourse to technical assistance as required.

Protection of children and young persons

Table 6.1 Instruments on the elimination of child labour (cont.)

Instruments	Number of ratifications (31 August 2002)	Status
Outdated instruments (cont.)		(Instruments that are no longer up to date; this category includes the Conventions that member States are no longer invited to ratify and the Recommendations whose implementation is no longer encouraged.)
Minimum Age (Industry) Convention (Revised), 1937 (No. 59)	15	The Governing Body has invited States parties to Convention No. 59 to contemplate ratifying the Minimum Age Convention, 1973 (No. 138), which would *ipso jure* involve the immediate denunciation of Convention No. 59 on the condition stated in Article 10(4)(a) of Convention No. 138, with recourse to technical assistance as required.
Minimum Age (Non-Industrial Employment) Convention (Revised), 1937 (No. 60)	1	The Governing Body shelved Convention No. 60 with immediate effect. It also invited the State party to Convention No. 60 to contemplate ratifying the Minimum Age Convention, 1973 (No. 138), and denouncing at the same time Convention No. 60. Finally, the Governing Body decided that the status of Convention No. 60 would be re-examined in due course with a view to its possible abrogation by the Conference.
Minimum Age (Underground Work) Convention, 1965 (No. 123)	25	The Governing Body has invited States parties to Convention No. 123 to contemplate ratifying the Minimum Age Convention, 1973 (No. 138), which would *ipso jure* involve the immediate denunciation of Convention No. 123 on the condition stated in Article 10(4)(f) of Convention No. 138, with recourse to technical assistance as required.
Minimum Age (Underground Work) Recommendation, 1965 (No. 124)	–	The Governing Body has noted that Recommendation No. 124 was obsolete and that this Recommendation should be withdrawn, while deferring the proposal to the Conference to withdraw the instrument until the situation has been re-examined at a later date.
Minimum Age (Coal Mines) Recommendation, 1953 (No. 96)	–	The Governing Body has noted that Recommendation No. 96 is obsolete and has decided to propose to the Conference the withdrawal of the Recommendation in due course.

Fundamental rights at work and international labour standards

Table 6.2 Instruments on the conditions of employment of young persons

Instruments	Number of ratifications (31 August 2002)	Status
Up-to-date instruments (Conventions whose ratification is encouraged and Recommendations to which member States are invited to give effect.)		
Medical Examination of Young Persons (Industry) Convention, 1946 (No. 77)	43	The Governing Body has invited member States to contemplate: (i) ratifying Conventions Nos. 77, 78 and 124 and to inform the Office of any obstacles or difficulties encountered that might prevent or delay the ratification of these Conventions; and (ii) the need for a full or partial revision of these Conventions, including their possible consolidation.
Medical Examination of Young Persons (Non-Industrial Occupations) Convention, 1946 (No. 78)	39	
Medical Examination of Young Persons (Underground Work) Convention, 1965 (No. 124)	41	
Medical Examination of Young Persons Recommendation, 1946 (No. 79)	–	The Governing Body has invited member States to give effect to Recommendations Nos. 79 and 125 and to inform the Office of any obstacles or difficulties encountered in the implementation of these Recommendations.
Conditions of Employment of Young Persons (Underground Work) Recommendation, 1965 (No. 125)	–	
Instruments to be revised (Instruments whose revision has been decided upon by the Governing Body.)		
Night Work of Young Persons (Industry) Convention, 1919 (No. 6)	59	The Governing Body has decided upon the revision of Conventions Nos. 6, 79 and 90 and Recommendations Nos. 14 and 80. These revisions are included in the item on night work of children and young persons, which is among the proposals for inclusion on the agenda of the Conference.
Night Work of Young Persons (Non-Industrial Occupations) Convention, 1946 (No. 79)	20	
Night Work of Young Persons (Industry) Convention (Revised), 1948 (No. 90)	50	
Night Work of Children and Young Persons (Agriculture) Recommendation, 1921 (No. 14)	–	
Night Work of Young Persons (Non-Industrial Occupations) Recommendation, 1946 (No. 80)	–	
Outdated instruments (Instruments that are no longer up to date; this category includes the Conventions that member States are no longer invited to ratify and the Recommendations whose implementation is no longer encouraged.)		
In the area of conditions of employment and work of children and young persons, no instrument has been considered as outdated by the Governing Body.		

Protection of children and young persons

Supervising the application of the system of medical examinations. In the great majority of cases, the Committee of Experts has recalled that identification measures are required to monitor the application of the system of medical examinations for fitness for employment of children and young persons working on their own account, or for their parents, in itinerant trading or in any other occupation carried on in the streets or in places to which the public has access.

(b) The Medical Examination of Young Persons (Underground Work) Convention, 1965 (No. 124)

(i) Scope of application of Convention No. 124

Convention No. 124 applies to employment or work underground in mines, including employment or work underground in quarries.[89] For the purpose of the application of the Convention, the term "mine" means any enterprise, whether public or private, for the extraction of any substance from under the surface of the earth by means involving the employment of persons underground.[90]

(ii) Medical examination

In the same way as Conventions Nos. 77 and 78, provision is also made in Convention No. 124 that a thorough medical examination, and periodic re-examinations at intervals of not more than one year, for fitness for employment shall be required for employment or work underground in mines.[91] These examinations are required for persons under 21 years of age. Nevertheless, alternative arrangements for medical supervision of young persons between 18 and 21 years are permitted where the competent authority is satisfied on medical advice that such arrangements are at least equivalent to those required, provided that the most representative organizations or employers and workers concerned have been consulted and have reached agreement.[92] The medical examinations have to be carried out under the responsibility and supervision of a qualified physician approved by the competent authority and have to be certified in an appropriate manner.[93]

As stipulated in Conventions Nos. 77 and 78, the medical examinations shall not involve the young persons, their parents or guardians, in any expense.[94]

(iii) Implementation of the instruments under examination

Medical examination for fitness for employment up to the age of 21 years

On several occasions, the Committee of Experts has drawn the attention of governments to the fact that Convention No. 124 requires a thorough medical examination for fitness for employment of persons under 21 years of age with a view to their employment or work underground in mines.

Fundamental rights at work and international labour standards

Medical examinations

On several occasions, the Committee of Experts has recalled that medical examinations have to be carried out under the responsibility and supervision of a qualified physician and certified in an appropriate manner. In the great majority of cases, it has also drawn the attention of governments to the fact that an X-ray film of the lungs must be required on the occasion of the initial medical examination and, when regarded as medically necessary, on the occasion of subsequent re-examinations.

Measures necessary for the enforcement of the Convention

In most cases, the Committee of Experts has recalled that records have to be maintained by employers and that the latter must make them available to inspectors. The records have to indicate the duly certified date of birth, the nature of the occupation and a certificate attesting fitness for employment. The Committee of Experts has sometimes drawn attention to the fact that records have to be made available to workers' representatives, at their request.

Consultation of organizations of employers and workers

On certain occasions, the Committee of Experts has drawn the attention of governments to the fact that the Convention requires that organizations of employers and workers be consulted before determining general policies for the implementation of the Convention and before adopting regulations to give effect to it.

Notes

[1] By "economic activity" is meant the production of goods and services as defined by the United Nations System of National Accounts. According to this system, the production of goods and services comprises: all production and processing of primary products, whether intended for the market, for exchange or for own consumption; production for the market of all other goods and services; and, in the case of the households producing such goods and services for the market, the corresponding production for own consumption. See on this subject the Labour Statistics Recommendation, 1985 (No. 170). See ILO: Governing Body, 264th Session, Geneva, Nov. 1995, doc. GB.264/ESP/1, p. 2, note 4.

[2] See doc. GB.264/ESP/1, para. 6. In this text, the term "child labour" covers all economic activities carried out by a child or young person. In general, these activities are covered by national laws and regulations, which must be in conformity with ILO instruments.

[3] These are: the Minimum Age (Industry) Convention, 1919 (No. 5); the Minimum Age (Sea) Convention, 1920 (No. 7); the Minimum Age (Agriculture) Convention, 1921 (No. 10); the Minimum Age (Trimmers and Stokers) Convention, 1921 (No. 15); the Minimum Age (Non-Industrial Employment) Convention, 1932 (No. 33); the Minimum Age (Sea) Convention (Revised), 1936 (No. 58); the Minimum Age (Industry) Convention (Revised), 1937 (No. 59); the Minimum Age (Non-Industrial Employment) Convention (Revised), 1937 (No. 60); the Minimum Age (Fishermen) Convention, 1959 (No. 112); the Minimum Age (Underground Work) Convention, 1965 (No. 123); the Minimum Age (Non-Industrial Employment) Recommendation, 1932 (No. 41); the Minimum Age (Family Undertakings) Recommendation,

Protection of children and young persons

1937 (No. 52); the Minimum Age (Coal Mines) Recommendation, 1953 (No. 96); and the Minimum Age (Underground Work) Recommendation, 1965 (No. 124).

[4] The Night Work of Young Persons (Industry) Convention, 1919 (No. 6); the Night Work of Young Persons (Non-Industrial Occupations) Convention, 1946 (No. 79); the Night Work of Young Persons (Industry) Convention (Revised), 1948 (No. 90); the Night Work of Young Persons (Non-Industrial Occupations) Recommendation, 1946 (No. 80); and the Night Work Recommendation, 1990 (No. 178).

[5] The Medical Examination of Young Persons (Sea) Convention, 1921 (No. 16); the Medical Examination of Young Persons (Industry) Convention, 1946 (No. 77); the Medical Examination of Young Persons (Non-Industrial Occupations) Convention, 1946 (No. 78); the Medical Examination of Young Persons (Underground Work) Convention, 1965 (No. 124); and the Medical Examination of Young Persons Recommendation, 1946 (No. 79). Moreover, the Conference has adopted seven Conventions and four Recommendations principally addressing other subjects, but which contain provisions on minimum age. See in this respect for hazardous and unhealthy work, the White Lead (Painting) Convention, 1921 (No. 13); the Radiation Protection Convention, 1960 (No. 115); the Maximum Weight Convention, 1967 (No. 127); the Benzene Convention, 1971 (No. 136); the Occupational Safety and Health (Dock Work) Convention, 1979 (No. 152); the Lead Poisoning (Women and Children) Recommendation, 1919 (No. 4); the Conditions of Employment of Young Persons (Underground Work) Recommendation, 1965 (No. 125); the Maximum Weight Recommendation, 1967 (No. 128); and the Benzene Recommendation, 1971 (No. 144). See also: the Social Policy (Non-Metropolitan Territories) Convention, 1947 (No. 82); the Social Policy (Basic Aims and Standards) Convention, 1962 (No. 117); the Seafarers' Hours of Work and the Manning of Ships Convention, 1996 (No. 180); and the Unemployment (Young Persons) Recommendation, 1935 (No. 45). In June 2001, at its 89th Session the Conference adopted the Safety and Health in Agriculture Convention (No. 184), and Recommendation (No. 192). These new instruments contained provisions on the safety and health of young workers. Article 16, para. 1, of Convention No. 184 provides that "[t]he minimum age for assignment to work in agriculture which by its nature or the circumstances in which it is carried out is likely to harm the safety and health of young persons shall not be less than 18 years".

[6] Indeed, many countries were not able to set, and particularly to apply, a minimum age for admission to employment or work in all sectors. This remains true today.

[7] ILO: *Minutes of the 181st Session of the Governing Body,* Geneva, 1970, Appendix II, para. 8.

[8] By way of illustration, reference may be made to the Declaration of the Rights of the Child, 1924, the Universal Declaration of Human Rights, 1948, the Declaration of the Rights of the Child, 1959, the International Covenant on Civil and Political Rights, 1966 and the International Covenant on Economic, Social and Cultural Rights, 1966.

[9] The Convention on the Rights of the Child is the most widely ratified international Convention by members of the United Nations. It has been ratified by 191 member States, and only the United States and Somalia have not yet ratified the Convention, although the United States has signed it. The Convention entered into force on 2 September 1990.

[10] IPEC's aim is the progressive elimination of child labour worldwide, emphasizing the eradication of the worst forms as rapidly as possible. It works to achieve this in several ways: through country-based programmes which promote policy reform and put in place concrete measures to end child labour; and through international and national campaigning intended to change social attitudes and promote the ratification and effective implementation of ILO Conventions on child labour. Complementing these efforts are in-depth research, legal expertise, policy analysis and programme evaluation carried out in the field at the regional and international levels. The political will and commitment of individual governments to address child labour – in alliance with employers' and workers' organizations, non-governmental organizations and other civil society actors – is the foundation for ILO-IPEC action. IPEC relies on a coalition of nearly 100 partners, comprising member countries that have invited IPEC to set up local programmes, donor governments and other contributing governmental and

non-governmental organizations. Since its inception in 1992, IPEC programmes in more than 60 countries have made a considerable impact in both removing hundreds of thousands of children from the workplace and raising general awareness of the scourge of child labour.

[11] Through the Declaration the ILO intends to provide a response to the challenges of economic globalization, which has been the subject of many debates within the Organization since 1994.

[12] See ILO: Governing Body ..., doc. GB.264/ESP/1, para. 81.

[13] ibid., para. 82.

[14] Conventions Nos. 5, 7, 10 and 33.

[15] Conventions Nos. 58, 59 and 60.

[16] Convention No. 123.

[17] Conventions Nos. 15, 115 and 136.

[18] These various possibilities are described below in the section on "Exceptions", pp. 98-100.

[19] ILO: *Minimum age for admission to employment*, Report IV(2), ILC, 58th Session, 1973, Geneva, p. 7.

[20] The Recommendation indicates that the commitment to full employment should be in accordance with the Employment Policy Convention (No. 122) and Recommendation (No. 122), 1964.

[21] L. Picard.: *La lutte contre le travail des enfants: cadre normatif* (Geneva, ILO, 1995), p. 2.

[22] ILO: *Minimum age for admission to employment*, 1973, op. cit., p. 7.

[23] ILO: *Record of Proceedings*, ILC, 57th Session, Geneva, 1972, No. 25 (Appendices: Fourth Item on the Agenda: Minimum Age of Admission to Employment), para. 21, p. 539.

[24] ILO: *Minimum age*, General Survey of the Reports relating to Convention No. 138 and Recommendation No. 146 concerning Minimum Age, Report of the Committee of Experts on the Application of Conventions and Recommendations, Report III (Part 4(B)), ILC, 67th Session, Geneva, 1981, para. 62.

[25] The link between minimum age and compulsory schooling has been emphasized since the creation of the ILO. See, ILC, 3rd Session, 1921, Vol. II, Third Part, Appendices and Index, Appendix XVIII, Report of the Director presented to the Conference, para. 252, p. 1052.

[26] Article 19 of Convention No. 82 and Article 15 of Convention No. 117 on social policy require that provision be made for the progressive development of broad systems of education, vocational training and apprenticeships.

[27] ILO: *Minimum age*, General Survey ..., 1981, op. cit., para. 140.

[28] It should be recalled that Article 6 of Conventions Nos. 33 and 60 provides that a higher age or ages shall be fixed "for admission of young persons and adolescents to employment for purposes of itinerant trading in the streets or in places to which the public have access, to regular employment at stalls outside shops or to employment in itinerant occupations, in cases where the conditions of such employment require that a higher age should be fixed". These provisions may prove to be useful where governments have to determine the types of employment that are hazardous. However, they do not explicitly state that these jobs are dangerous. Paragraph 6 of the Minimum Age (Non-Industrial Employment) Recommendation, 1932 (No. 41), indicates that dangerous employment might include certain employment in public entertainments such as acrobatic performances; in establishments for the cure of the sick such as employment involving danger of contagion or infection; and in establishments for the sale of alcoholic liquor such as serving customers.

[29] The Minimum Age (Agriculture) Convention, 1921 (No. 10), was the first Convention to set a minimum age for admission to employment or work that was lower than the general minimum age in the case of "light work". It places the concept of "light work" in the

Protection of children and young persons

context of vocational instruction. Its provisions on this subject therefore differ from those of Convention No. 138 of 1973. See ILO: *Minimum age,* General Survey ..., 1981, op. cit., para. 154. The Minimum Age (Non-Industrial Employment) Convention, 1932 (No. 33), and the Minimum Age (Non-Industrial Employment) Convention (Revised), 1937 (No. 60), also provide that an age lower than the general minimum age may be specified for "light work". However, these Conventions contain standards which are more complex and detailed on this subject than Convention No. 138. They explicitly set out the hours and days when such work is authorized, and also limit the possibilities of employing children who are still engaged in compulsory school during the holidays.

[30] Examples of types of work considered to be light are given in Paragraph 2 of the Minimum Age (Non-Industrial Employment) Recommendation, 1932 (No. 41): running errands, distribution of newspapers, odd jobs in connection with the practice of sports or the playing of games, and picking and selling flowers or fruits. For the admission of children to light work, in accordance with the Recommendation, the consent of parents or guardians, a medical certificate of physical fitness and, "where necessary, previous consultation with the school authorities" should be required. The hours of work should be adapted to the school timetable and the age of the child.

[31] As permitted by Article 2, para. 4, of Convention No. 138 for States whose economy and educational facilities are insufficiently developed.

[32] ILO: *Minimum Age,* General Survey ..., 1981, op. cit., para. 75.

[33] See section 6.2.1(a)(iv), "Establishment of a higher minimum age for admission to work that is likely to jeopardize the health, safety or morals", above.

[34] Article 5, para. 1.

[35] Article 5, para. 2.

[36] Article 5, para. 4(a).

[37] The earlier Conventions on the minimum age for admission to employment or work address a single aspect of this issue, namely work carried out in vocational training institutions. Conventions Nos. 5, 7, 10, 15, 58, 59 and 112 exclude from their application work done by children in technical schools and school-ships or training ships, provided that such work is approved and supervised by public authority. Conventions No. 33 and 60 contain more detailed provisions on vocational training with a view to employment or work in non-industrial activities and, under certain conditions, do not apply to work done in technical schools.

[38] Conventions Nos. 33 and 60 on the minimum age for admission to employment in non-industrial work contain much more detailed and restrictive provisions than Convention No. 138. For example, see Article 4.

[39] ILO: *Minimum age for admission to employment,* 1973, op. cit., p. 21.

[40] Picard, op. cit., p. 7.

[41] This point takes into account the provisions of the Conventions on the night work of young persons.

[42] The obligation to make effective ratified Conventions is set out in article 19, para. 5(d), of the Constitution. The formal obligation is set out in article 22 of the Constitution, which requires member States to provide reports on the application of ratified Conventions.

[43] With regard to the national policy, see 6.2.1(a)(ii), above.

[44] Several ILO instruments address the subject of labour inspection. See the Labour Inspection Convention, 1947 (No. 81) [Protocol of 1995 to the Labour Inspection Convention, 1947]; the Labour Inspection Recommendation, 1947 (No. 81); and the Labour Inspection (Agriculture) Convention (No. 129) and Recommendation (No. 133), 1969. Under the terms of these instruments, the functions of the system of labour inspection shall be "to secure the enforcement of the legal provisions relating to [...] the employment of children and young persons, and other connected matters, in so far as such provisions are enforceable by labour inspectors". See Article 3, para. 1(a), of Convention No. 81 and Article 6, para. 1(a), of Convention No. 129.

Fundamental rights at work and international labour standards

[45] ILO: *Minimum age,* General Survey ..., 1981, op. cit., para. 328.

[46] ibid., para. 332.

[47] Unless the minimum age for admission to employment or work has been set at 14 years of age. In this case, in accordance with Article 2, para. 4, the age range for light work is between 12 and 14 years.

[48] These discussions were held in the Employment and Social Policy Committee of the Governing Body. See ILO: Governing Body, 264th Session, Geneva, Nov. 1995, docs. GB.264/ESP/1, GB.264/10, paras. 25-62, and GB.264/2, paras. 12-21.

[49] ibid., 265th Session, Mar. 1996, docs. GB.265/2, paras. 8-53, and GB.265/205. Discussions were also held at the Informal Tripartite Meeting at the Ministerial Level and at the Conference in June 1996.

[50] L. Picard. "Why new international instruments on child labour?", in *Labour Education*, 1997/3, No. 108 (Geneva, ILO).

[51] ILO: *Child labour*, Report IV(2A), ILC, 87th Session, Geneva, 1999, Office commentary, p. 19-20.

[52] ibid., p. 34.

[53] ibid.

[54] ibid.

[55] ibid., Office commentary, p. 39.

[56] Indeed, the forms of slavery or practices similar to slavery referred to in Article 3(a) of Convention No. 182 are covered by Convention No. 29. The use, procuring or offering of a child for purposes such as prostitution referred to in Article 3(b) of Convention No. 182 are considered by the Committee of Experts to be forms of forced labour under Convention No. 29.

[57] ILO: *Child labour: Targeting the intolerable*, Report VI(1), ILC, 86th Session, Geneva, 1998, p. 66.

[58] ILO: *Record of Proceedings*, ILC, 87th Session, Geneva, 1999, Report of the Committee on Child Labour, para. 136, p. 19/31. For the definition of forced labour, see Chapter 4.

[59] Particularly the International Agreement for the suppression of the "white slave trade", 1904; the International Convention for the Suppression of Traffic in Women and Children, 1921; the Slavery Convention, 1926; the Protocol amending the Slavery Convention of 1926; and the Supplementary Convention on the Abolition of Slavery, the Slave Trade, and Institutions and Practices Similar to Slavery, 1956.

[60] As confirmed by the Office at the request of the Government of Canada. See ILO: *Child labour,* Report IV(2A), 1999, op. cit., Office commentary, p. 60. With regard to the trafficking of children, it should be noted that on 1 November 2000, the General Assembly of the United Nations adopted the Convention against Transnational Organized Crime, 2000, as well as its additional Protocol to Prevent, Suppress and Punish Trafficking in Persons, Especially Women and Children, 2000.

[61] ILO, *Record of Proceedings*, 1999, op. cit., paras. 141 and 143, pp. 19/32 and 33. On 25 May 2000, the United Nations General Assembly adopted, without a vote, the Optional Protocol to the Convention on the Rights of the Child on the involvement of children in armed conflicts.

[62] On 25 May 2000, the General Assembly of the United Nations adopted without a vote the Optional Protocol to the Convention on the Rights of the Child on the sale of children, child prostitution and child pornography. The Convention for the Suppression of the Traffic in Persons and of the Exploitation of the Prostitution of Others, 1949, may also be taken into consideration. The Rome Statute of the International Criminal Court, adopted in 1998 by a United Nations Conference of Plenipotentiaries, affords additional protection to children involved in armed conflict.

[63] ILO, *Child labour*, Report VI(2), ILC, 86th Session, Geneva, 1998, p. 52. In this respect, it should be noted that Article 2 to the Optional Protocol to the Convention on the Rights

Protection of children and young persons

of the Child on the sale of children, child prostitution and child pornography, provides that, for the purposes of the Protocol: (a) sale of children means any act or transaction whereby a child is transferred by any person or group of persons to another for remuneration or any other consideration; (b) child prostitution means the use of a child in sexual activities for remuneration or any other consideration; (c) child pornography means any representation, by whatever means, of a child engaged in real or simulated explicit sexual activities or any representation of the sexual parts of a child for primarily sexual purposes.

[64] ILO: *Child labour*, Report IV(2A), 1999, op. cit., Office commentary, pp. 60 and 61.

[65] The Office views the relevant treaties as being the following: the Single Convention on Narcotic Drugs, 1961; the Convention on Psychotropic Substances, 1971; the Protocol amending the Single Convention on Narcotic Drugs, 1972; and the United Nations Convention against Illicit Traffic in Narcotic Drugs and Psychotropic Substances, 1988. See, on this subject, ILO: *Child labour*, Report IV(2A), 1999, op. cit., Office commentary, p. 61. Article 3(c) of Convention No. 182 recalls Article 33 of the Convention on the Rights of the Child, which provides that "States Parties shall take all appropriate measures, including legislative, administrative, social and educational measures, to protect children from the illicit use of narcotic drugs and psychotropic substances as defined in the relevant international treaties, and to prevent the use of children in the illicit production and trafficking of such substances".

[66] ILO: *Child labour*, Report IV(2A), 1999, op. cit., p. 62.

[67] International labour Conventions or United Nations Conventions.

[68] International labour Recommendations. On this subject, see ILO: *Child Labour*, Report IV(2A), 1999, op. cit., Office commentary, p. 77.

[69] ibid., pp. 65 and 66.

[70] ILO: *Record of Proceedings*, 1999, op. cit., para. 194, p. 19/42.

[71] ILO: *Child labour*, Report IV(2A), 1999, op. cit., p. 80.

[72] ILO: *Record of Proceedings*, 1999, op. cit., para. 143, p. 19/33. A number of other Conventions, such as the Vocational Rehabilitation and Employment (Disabled Persons) Convention, 1983 (No. 159), and the Minimum Wage Fixing Convention, 1970 (No. 131), include similar references to other concerned groups or competent persons.

[73] ILO: *Child labour*, Report IV(2A), 1999, op. cit., Office commentary, p. 98.

[74] See the comments concerning Article 1 of Convention No. 182.

[75] ILO: *Child labour*, Report IV(2A), 1999, op. cit., pp. 34-35.

[76] ILO: *Record of Proceedings*, 1999, op. cit., para. 242, p. 19/49.

[77] ibid, para. 243, p. 19/49.

[78] Article 1, para. 1, of Convention No. 77.

[79] Article 1, paras. 1 and 2, of Convention No. 78.

[80] Article 1, para. 4, of Convention No. 78.

[81] Article 2, para. 1, of Conventions Nos. 77 and 78.

[82] Article 2, para. 2, of Conventions Nos. 77 and 78. Under the terms of para. 3, the document certifying fitness for employment may be issued subject to specified conditions of employment and issued for a specified job or for a group of jobs or occupations involving similar health risks which have been classified as a group by the authority responsible for the enforcement of the laws and regulations concerning medical examinations for fitness for employment.

[83] Article 4, para. 1, of Conventions Nos. 77 and 78. Article 4, para. 2, of the Conventions provides that national laws or regulations shall either specify, or empower an appropriate authority to specify, the occupations or categories of occupations in which medical examination and re-examinations for fitness for employment shall be required until at least the age of 21 years.

[84] Article 5 of Conventions Nos. 77 and 78.

[85] Article 3, para. 1, of Conventions Nos. 77 and 78.

Fundamental rights at work and international labour standards

[86] Article 3, para. 2, of Conventions Nos. 77 and 78.
[87] Article 4, para. 1, of Conventions Nos. 77 and 78. See note 83 above.
[88] Article 3, para. 3, of Conventions Nos. 77 and 78.
[89] Article 1, para. 2.
[90] Article 1, para. 1.
[91] Article 2, para. 1.
[92] Article 2, para. 2.
[93] Article 3, para. 1.
[94] Article 3, para. 3.

GLOSSARY

International Labour Conference (ILC). Supreme body of the ILO. Meets once a year in the month of June and gathers together governments and employers' and workers' organizations from each of the 175 member States of the ILO (tripartism). Adopts the ILO budget and international labour Conventions and Recommendations, and determines the Organization's policy and programmes.

Governing Body. Executive body of the ILO (tripartite). Elects the Director-General of the Office, prepares the Organization's programme and budget, sets the agenda of the Conference, determines the Organization's standards policy and its technical cooperation policy, supervises the implementation of related programmes and implements the decisions of the Conference.

International labour Conventions. Instruments intended to create international obligations upon States which ratify them.

International labour Recommendations. Instruments providing guidance for action by governments and employers' and workers' organizations; they are not intended to give rise to obligations, nor can they be ratified by member States.

Committee of Experts on the Application of Conventions and Recommendations. Established by the Governing Body in 1926 to examine government reports on the application of Conventions and other obligations contained in the ILO Constitution relating to international labour standards; assesses the conformity of national law and practice with the provisions of ILO Conventions. Composed of 20 high-level jurists (judges of supreme courts, professors, legal experts, etc.) appointed by the Governing Body. It meets once a year in November-December and its report is examined by the International Labour Conference.

Committee on the Application of Standards. Tripartite Committee of the International Labour Conference which takes as a basis for its work the report of the Committee of Experts. In its report to the Conference, the Committee on the Application of Standards makes conclusions, inviting the governments concerned to provide clarifications and take measures, where appropriate, to overcome divergencies observed between national law and practice and the provisions of ratified Conventions.

General Surveys of the Committee of Experts. Drawn up on the basis of the reports received from governments and employers' and workers' organizations following requests by the Governing Body concerning the situation of national law and practice in relation to one or more Conventions and Recommendations. Provides a comparative description of the situation of national law and practice in relation to the instruments under consideration and establishes the main lines for the application of these instruments.

Observations. Comments by the Committee of Experts published in its report. An observation is normally made in the most serious or long-lasting cases of non-compliance with obligations.

Direct requests. Comments by the Committee of Experts which are not published in its report, but are sent to governments by the Office on behalf of the Committee of Experts. Direct requests generally raise technical issues, and may also request clarifications on certain points.

BIBLIOGRAPHICAL REFERENCES AND INTERNET SITES

REGULAR INTERNATIONAL LABOUR STANDARDS PUBLICATIONS

ILO Conventions and Recommendations. Available in bound edition (three volumes, 1919-95), with separate offprints of subsequent instruments.

Report of the Committee of Experts. Published annually. Report III(1A) contains general and individual observations concerning particular countries. Part III(1B) contains the General Survey, which examines the application in law and practice of a particular set of Conventions and Recommendations in ILO member States. Part III(2) contains a list of ratifications of ILO Conventions.

Report of the Committee on the Application of Standards. Published annually in the *Provisional Record* of the International Labour Conference.

ILOLEX CD-ROM. Published biannually. Database of ILO standards. Includes Conventions, Recommendations, reports of the Committee of Experts, reports of the Committee on Freedom of Association, General Surveys, and numerous related documents. Also available at the ILO web site at www.ilo.org

International Labour Standards Electronic Library (ILSE CD-ROM). Contains a browse version of basic international labour standards documents. Updated annually.

GENERAL WORKS

Bartolomei De La Cruz, H.; von Potobsky, G.; Swepston, L.: *International Labour Organization: The international standards system and basic human rights* (Boulder, CO, Westview Press, 1996).

Bonvin, M.: *L'Organisation internationale du Travail: Étude sur une agence productrice de normes* (Paris, Presses universitaires de France, 1998).

Gladstone, A.: "The manager's guide to international labour standards", in *Management Development Series*, No. 23 (Geneva, ILO, 1986).

ILO: "Comparative analysis of the International Covenants on Human Rights and International Labour Conventions and Recommendations", in *Official Bulletin*, Vol. LII, 1969, No. 2, pp. 181-216.

—: *Constitution of the International Labour Organisation*, 1998.

—: *Handbook of procedures relating to international labour Conventions and Recommendations*, 2nd revised edition (Geneva, International Labour Standards Department, 1998).

—: *International labour standards: A worker's education manual*, 4th revised edition (Geneva, 1998).

Fundamental rights at work and international labour standards

—: *Labour rights, international labour standards and international trade* (Turin, International Training Centre, 1996).
—: Report of the Organization for Economic Cooperation and Development on trade, employment and labour standards, document GB.267/WP/SDL/2 (Nov. 1996).
—: *Trade union participation in the ILO supervisory system for the protection of trade union rights* (Geneva, 1996).
—: *International labour standards and development: A trainer's guide* (Turin, International Training Centre, 1992).
—: *The impact of international labour Conventions and Recommendations* (Geneva, 1990).
—: *International labour standards for development and social justice* (Geneva, Nov. 1989).
—: *International standards and guiding principles on labour laws and labour relations*, No. 74, 1989.
—: *Human rights: A common responsibility*, Labour-Management Relations Series, Report of the Director-General (I), International Labour Conference, 75th Session (Geneva, 1988).
—: *International labour standards*, Report of the Director-General (I), International Labour Conference, 70th Session (Geneva, 1984).
Kellerson, H.: "The ILO Declaration of 1998 on fundamental principles and rights: A challenge for the future", in *International Labour Review*, Vol. 137, No. 2 (1998) (Special issue), pp. 223-235.
Lee, E.: "Globalization and labour standards: A review of issues", in *International Labour Review*, Vol. 136, No. 2 (1997), pp. 173-189.
OECD: *International trade and core labour standards* (Paris, 2000).
Plant, R.: *Labour standards and structural adjustment* (Geneva, ILO, 1994).
Polites, G.: *International labour standards: The process of adoption and supervision*, ACT/EMP/9 (Geneva, ILO, 1990).
Reynaud, A.: *Labour standards and the integration process in the Americas* (Geneva, ILO, 2001).
Sengenberger, W.; Campbell, D. (eds.): *International labour standards and economic interdependence: Essays in commemoration of the 75th anniversary of the International Labour Organization and the 50th anniversary of the Declaration of Philadelphia* (Geneva, ILO, 1994).
Swepston, L.: "Supervision of ILO standards", in *International Journal of Comparative Labour Law and Industrial Relations*, Vol. 13, No. 4 (1997), pp. 327-344.
Swinnerton, K.A.: "Essay on economic efficiency and core labour standards", in *World Economy*, 20(1) (Jan. 1997), pp. 73-86.
Valticos, N.: "Once more about the ILO system of supervision: In what respect is it still a model?", in *Towards more effective supervision by international organizations* (Groningen, Martinus Nijhoff Publications, 1994), pp. 99-113.
—; von Potobsky, G.: *International labour law*, 2nd edition (Deventer, Kluwer Law and Taxation Publishers, 1995).

FREEDOM OF ASSOCIATION, COLLECTIVE BARGAINING AND INDUSTRIAL RELATIONS

Dunning, H.: "The origins of Convention No. 87 on freedom of association and the right to organize", in *International Labour Review*, Vol. 137, No. 2 (1998), pp. 149-167.
Gernigon, B.; Odero, A.; Guido, H.: *Collective bargaining: ILO standards and the principles of the supervisory bodies* (Geneva, ILO, 2000).
—; —; —: "ILO principles concerning collective bargaining", in *International Labour Review*, Vol. 139, No. 1, 2000, pp. 37-60.

Bibliographical references and Internet sites

Gravel, E.; Duplessis, I.; Gernigon, B.: *The Committee on Freedom of Association: Its impact over 50 years* (Geneva, ILO, 2001).

Heron, R.; Vaandenabeele, C.: *Tripartism: An introductory guide* (Bangkok, ILO East Asia Multidisciplinary Advisory Team, 1998).

Hodges-Aeberhard, J.: "Right to organize in Article 2 of Convention No. 87: What is meant by workers without distinction whatsoever?", in *International Labour Review*, Vol. 128, No. 2, 1989, pp. 177-194.

ILO: *Tripartite consultation: General Survey on the Tripartite Consultation (International Labour Standards) Convention, 1976 (No. 144) and the Tripartite Consultation (Activities of the International Labour Organisation) Recommendation, 1976 (No. 152)*, Report III (1B), International Labour Conference, 88th Session, Geneva, 2000.

—: *Your voice at work: Global Report under the follow-up to the ILO Declaration on Fundamental Principles and Rights at Work*, Report of the Director-General, International Labour Conference, 88th Session, 2000.

—: *Freedom of association: An annotated bibliography* (Geneva, 1999).

—: *Multinational enterprises and social policy: Reflections on twenty years of the Tripartite Declaration* (Geneva, Multinational Enterprises Branch, 1999).

—: *Tripartism and social dialogue: Prerequisites for social and economic development: An overview* (Geneva, 1999.)

—: *Freedom of association: Digest of decisions and principles of the Freedom of Association Committee of the Governing Body of the ILO*, 4th edition (Geneva, 1996).

—: *ILO law on freedom of association: Standards and procedures* (Geneva, 1996).

—: *Tripartite consultation at the national level on economic and social policy*, Report VI, International Labour Conference, 83rd Session, Geneva, 1996.

—: *Tripartismo y las normas internacionales del trabajo* (Geneva, 1995).

—: *Freedom of association and collective bargaining: General Survey of the Reports on the Freedom of Association and the Right to Organise Convention, 1948 (No. 87), and the Right to Organise and Collective Bargaining Convention, 1949 (No. 98)*, Report III(4B), International Labour Conference, 81st Session, Geneva, 1994.

—: *Structure and functions of rural workers' organizations: A workers' education manual*, 2nd (revised) edition (Geneva, 1990).

—: *Trade unions and the ILO: A workers' education manual*, 2nd edition (Geneva, 1990).

—: *Principles, standards and procedures concerning freedom of association* (Geneva, 1986).

—: *Industrial relations and tripartism: Structural change, dialogue and social progress*, Report of the Director-General (I), International Labour Conference, 71st Session, Geneva, 1985.

—: *Tripartite consultation: General Survey of the Reports relating to Convention No. 144 and Recommendation No. 152*, Report III(4B), International Labour Conference, 68th Session, Geneva, 1982.

Javillier, J.-C.: *Conférences de l'OIT sur la politique sociale: L'évolution des relations professionnelles et du droit du travail dans un monde en changement* (Geneva, International Institute for Labour Studies, 1996).

Swepston, L.: "Human rights law and freedom of association: Development through ILO supervision", in *International Labour Review*, Vol. 137, No. 2 (1998) (Special issue), pp. 169-194.

Trebilcock, A.: *Towards social dialogue: Tripartite cooperation in national economic and social policy-making* (Geneva, ILO, 1994).

von Potobsky, G.: "Freedom of association: The impact of Convention No. 87 and ILO action", in *International Labour Review*, Vol. 137, No. 2 (1998) (Special issue), pp. 195-221.

Fundamental rights at work and international labour standards

FORCED LABOUR

ILO: *Stopping forced labour: Global Report under the Follow-up to the ILO Declaration on Fundamental Principles and Rights at Work*, Report of the Director-General, International Labour Conference, 89th Session, 2001.

—: "Report of the Commission of Inquiry appointed under article 26 of the Constitution of the International Labour Organization to examine the observance by Myanmar of the Forced Labour Convention (No. 29), 1930", in *Official Bulletin*, Special Supplement, Vol. LXXXI, Series B, 1998.

—: "Report of the Commission of Inquiry appointed under article 26 of the Constitution of the International Labour Organization to examine the observance of certain international labour Conventions by the Dominican Republic", in *Official Bulletin*, Special Supplement, Vol. LXVI, Series B, 1983.

—: *Abolition of forced labour: General Survey of the Reports on the Forced Labour Convention, 1930 (No. 29), and the Abolition of Forced Labour Convention, 1957 (No. 105)*, Report III (4B), International Labour Conference, 65th Session, 1979.

—: "Prison labour", in *International Labour Review*, Vol. XXV, Nos. 3 and 4, 1932, pp. 311-331 and 499-524.

EQUALITY OF OPPORTUNITY AND TREATMENT

ILO: *Decent work for women: The ILO's contribution to Women 2000: Gender equality, development and peace for the twenty-first century*, Governing Body, 277th Session, Geneva, March 2000.

—: *Equality in employment and occupation: Special Survey on equality in employment and occupation in respect of Convention No. 111*, Report III(4B), International Labour Conference, 83rd Session, Geneva, 1996.

—: *International labour standards and women workers' rights: Trainer's guide* (Geneva, 1994).

—: *Women and work: Selected ILO policy documents* (Geneva, 1994).

—: *Equality in employment and occupation: General Survey of the Reports on the Discrimination (Employment and Occupation) Convention (No. 111) and Recommendation (No. 111), 1958*, Report III(4B), International Labour Conference, 75th Session, Geneva, 1988.

—: *Equal remuneration: General Survey of the Reports on the Equal Remuneration Convention (No. 111), 1958 and Recommendation (No. 90), 1951*, Report III(4B), International Labour Conference, 72nd Session, Geneva, 1986.

CHILDREN AND ADOLESCENTS

Grootaert, C.; Kanbur, R.: "Child labour: An economic perspective", in *International Labour Review*, Vol. 134, No. 2 (1995), pp. 187-203.

ILO: *A future without child labour: Global Report under the Follow-up to the ILO Declaration on Fundamental Principles and Rights at Work*, Report of the Director-General, International Labour Conference, 90th Session, 2002.

—: *Child labour: Targeting the intolerable*, Report VI(1), International Labour Conference, 86th Session, 1998.

—: *Child labour: What is to be done?*, Record of Proceedings of the Informal Tripartite Meeting at the Ministerial Level (Geneva, 1996).

—: "Trade unions and child labour", in *Labour Education*, 1996/1, No. 102, pp. 1-55.

Bibliographical references and Internet sites

—: *Minimum age: General Survey of the Reports relating to Convention No. 138 and Recommendation No. 146 concerning minimum age*, Report III(4B), International Labour Conference, 67th Session, Geneva, 1981.

—: *Minimum age for admission to employment*, Report IV(1) and (2), International Labour Conference, 57th and 58th Sessions, 1972 and 1973.

Lansky, M.: *Child labour: How the challenge is being met* (Geneva, IPEC, 1998).

Picard, L.: *La lutte contre le travail des enfants* (Geneva, ILO, 1995).

—: "Why new international instruments on child labour?", in *Labour Education*, 1997/3, No. 108 (Geneva).

INTERNET RESOURCES

ILO sites

Web site of the International Labour Organization: http://www.ilo.org
ILO Declaration on Fundamental Principles and Rights at Work:
    http://www.ilo.org/public/english/standards/decl
ILOLEX: (Trilingual database (English, French, Spanish) on international labour standards):
    http://www.ilo.org/ilolex/english/index.htm
InFocus Programme on Strengthening Social Dialogue:
    http://www.ilo.org/public/english/dialogue/ifpdial/intro/index.htm

Other sites

European Industrial Relations Observatory (EIRO): http://www.eiro.eurofound.ie
European Trade Union Confederation: http://www.etuc.org
European Union (EU): http://www.europa.eu.int
International Confederation of Free Trade Unions (ICFTU): http://www.icftu.org
International Maritime Organization: http://www.imo.org
International Organisation of Employers (IOE): http://www.ioe-emp.org
International Organization for Migration: http://www.iom.int
International Social Security Association: http://www.issa.int
MERCOSUR: http://www.mercosur.org.uy
NAFTA secretariat: http://www.nafta-sec-alena.org
Office of the High Commissioner for Human Rights: http://www.unhchr.ch
World Confederation of Labour: http://www.cmt-wcl.org
World Federation of Trade Unions (WFTU): http://www.wftu.cz